A history of Frank C. Strick and his many shipping enterprises

by

J. E. B. Belt
and
H. S. Appleyard

Published by the World Ship Society
Kendal LA9 7LT
1996

H. S. Appleyard

CONTENTS

ISBN 0 905617 81 9

FRANK CLARKE STRICK

In a lifetime in shipping, Mr. Strick became an almost legendary figure. From his early days in Swansea, where he first made a name for himself in business circles, he had gradually built an empire. Always ready to grasp an opportunity and being gifted with an expertise in financial matters, he launched into new ventures whenever an opportunity arose.

The many activities with which he became involved were spread around the ports of the United Kingdom, Holland, Belgium and France. From Gibraltar and the countries bordering the Mediterranean to Egypt, his name was known and respected, not only because of his fleets of ships, but also his coal bunkering enterprises,

These bunkering facilities were, the British Coaling Depots Limited at Port Said, The Algiers Bunkering Company Limited, and the Oran Coal Co. Ltd. The British Coaling Depots Ltd. also operated a depot at Port Sudan, where they not only provided a ship bunkering service but also imported coal for the Sudan Railways.

Oran, particularly, owed to him, it's development as one of the greatest coal bunkering ports, and his own interests alone were at one time handling over 300,000 tons per year. The facilities owned by the company at Oran consisted of two overhead transporter cranes carrying grabs, and a fleet of flat topped barges towed by tugs carrying the chevron funnel mark.

British Coaling Depots Ltd., was formed in 1909 and provided a coal bunkering service at Port Said and Suez, and later a ship's agency service. Various other facilties were supplied by the company and they were similar to those provided by The English Coaling Co. which was owned by the P&O Steam Navigation Company. In 1928, when Mr. Strick acquired his 49% interest in Strick Line Ltd. from P&O these two companies were combined to form The Suez Canal Ligherage Co. Ltd. with Strick owning 49% and P&O the 51% controlling interest. This company provided a service of lighterage, tugs, workshops, supply and maintenance of canal searchlights and agency work. These businesses remained in operation until 1964, when they were put into liquidation after the Egyptian government had nationalised all the assets.

Much of the coal for the Mediterranean bunkering stations was shipped out of South Wales and North East Coast ports, and it was estimated that vessels managed by Strick carried something like a million tons of coal outwards annually and a similar amount of iron ore homewards. In addition, large quantities of coal were at one time shipped to Karachi for the account of the India Office.

Mr. Strick also had interests in the Mokta-al-Hadad iron ore mines in North Africa.

Despite all these interests it was in the Persian Gulf, where he was a pioneer in the trade that Mr. Strick had his most important success. A major part of his prosperity was provided by the shipping services to the countries bordering the Gulf, and the import/export business in Iraq and Iran.

From a first tentative step, with one small ship, he worked and expanded his shipping services until, together with his associates, he had interests in three large fleets, a large trading business in the Gulf, coal bunkering and ancillary services in the Suez Canal and Red Sea, and major bunkering facilities and coal business in the Mediterranean.

He remained a bachelor all his life, and it seems a pity that such a man should have no family to carry on after him. It is interesting that he never visited the Persian Gulf.

COMPANY HISTORY

Frank Clarke Strick was born in Swansea in October 1849, the third child of James Strick, a shipbroker and Lloyds Agent of that port. James Strick was also a shipowner in a small way. He had, during the 1860's, at least two brigantines built, each of about 220 tons, and employed them in the coal trade from South Wales to West of England ports.

Frank Strick's first employment was in a local bank, where he undoubtedly learned the basic principles of business and finance which would be of great value to him in later years. Before long he left the bank and joined his father's business, where he gained valuable experience as a shipbroker before leaving to join the firm of Poingdestre, Mesnier & Co., coal exporters and chartering agents, as a junior partner. Here, he acquired the comprehensive knowledge of the coal trade which was eventually to make him such a powerful influence in the Mediterranean bunkering business, and also made friendships which were to be of great importance in his future as a businessman.

Apart from coal exporting, Poingdestre, Mesnier & Co. were associated with other companies in the selling and shipping of iron ore from North Africa. One of these companies was the Mokta Company of Paris, a great power in the ore business which would later have an effect on his career. After some time in Swansea with Poingdestre, Mesnier & Co., Mr. Strick decided to go into business for himself and on the 20th October 1885, he set up as a shipbroker and coal exporter under the name of Frank C. Strick & Co. Ltd. in Woolpack Buildings, Gracechurch Street, London. The subscribers to the association being mainly family members. About this time M. Poingdestre retired and M. Mesnier returned to his native Paris, where he too formed his own company, called Societe Commerciale D'Affretements et de Commission.

In 1887, Mr. Strick decided to try shipowning and bought a vessel, the NORMAND, which had in fact been ordered by his friend M. Mesnier. After operating the NORMAND for only a year he sold her in order to help finance a larger vessel and, in association with Jules Mesnier of Paris, he founded London & Paris Steamship Co. Ltd. The directors being Mon. S. Santerre (Chairman), F. C. Strick, M. J. Mesnier, M. F. Gorches, F. Japp, F. Jonas and J. Holmes.

The new vessel, built in 1889, cost £23,250 and was named ALPHONSE PARRAN, the name of the chairman of the Mokta Company. A new company was formed to operate the vessel, called Anglo-Algerian Steamship Co. Ltd. and she was employed in the coal trade from South Wales to Northern France, together with chartered tonnage as required.

Some time later, through M. Mesnier's connection with the Mokta Company, Mr. Strick obtained a contract to carry coal to Mediterranean ports and return with iron ore from North Africa and he again chartered a number of vessels to provide the service. About this time, Mr. Strick moved his office to Bishopsgate House in Bishopsgate.

It is thought that because of his earlier experience of shipping coal to the Persian Gulf bunkering stations, M. Mesnier encouraged Mr. Strick to send the ALPHONSE PARRAN to the Gulf with coal and some general cargo to sound out the prospects. The results of this voyage in 1892 were so good that Mr. Strick decided to form a new company, called the Anglo-Arabian and Persian Steamship Co. Ltd., with M. Mesnier as one of the directors, and to have ships built for the trade. The first ship built for this new company was the ARABISTAN in 1893. She had twin funnels and was registered at Swansea, as were all the ships for many years afterwards.

The basis of the new trade was bunker coal to the depots at Bushire and Basrah, for the use of the vessels calling, mainly on the India-Gulf run. The British India Steam Navigation Co. Ltd. had been operating in this trade since the 1850's and the main reason for founding the new company was to encourage local business men in the Gulf to become shareholders and so help develop trade in both directions. Many merchants did become shareholders and trade increased to such an extent that in the next eleven years nine vessels were added to the fleet of Anglo-Arabian & Persian Steamship Co. Ltd. The names of the ships were place names in Persia and surrounding area, ending in 'ISTAN which means 'land of' in Pharsee, the Persian language.

In 1896, the Anglo-Algerian Steamship Co. Ltd. went into voluntary liquidation and Mr. Strick formed a new company, Anglo-Algerian Steamship Co. (1896) Ltd. with M. Jules Mesnier as chairman. This new firm was to run the ever expanding coal and iron ore trade to and from the Mediterranean and also provide ships to assist when necessary in the Gulf trade. The ALPHONSE PARRAN was transferred to the new company. The first vessel built for Anglo-Algerian Steamship Co. (1896) Ltd. was the BALUCHISTAN by William Gray & Co. Ltd. of West Hartlepool, who, from then on until 1927 built the great majority of Strick vessels.

The entrance to the Shatt-el-Arab river, like many great deltas, is hampered by a bar, caused by the vast amount of silt bought down, and at that time the maximum draught for a ship to cross was about twenty feet. Trade was expanding and Mr. Strick wanted to use larger vessels with draughts greater than 20 feet, so he conceived the idea of keeping small ships on station which could lighten larger vessels and enable them to deliver a full cargo direct to river ports. To this end he bought the DWINA in 1895 and the ESTHER in 1901. They were stationed permanently on the river where they met incoming ocean going vessels and transferred part cargo before both vessels then proceded over the bar to the destination. This lightening procedure was used continuously until 1926 when the dredging of a proper channel was completed and ships were able to carry a full cargo direct to Basrah over both the Rooka bar at the river entrance and the Karun bar just below Khorramshahr.

In those early days there was no local labour force at Basrah and all vessels bound up river called at Bushire to embark a pilot, and up to a hundred labourers who lived on board until the ship completed her discharging and loading in the river and called back at Bushire to land them. This practice continued right up to the 1930's.

By the turn of the century Mr. Strick had fifteen ships in his various companies and had offices in London, Swansea, Cardiff, Newport, Newcastle and Manchester. The London & Paris Steamship Co. Ltd. had commenced building ships in 1897, the first being the PARIS, and they were engaged on the bunker coal run from South Wales to Le Havre where their cargoes fueled the passenger liners of Cie. Generale Transatlantique.

In 1903 F. C. Strick entered into a working agreement with the Bucknall Steamship Lines (later Ellerman and Bucknall) to provide a joint service to the Gulf and Bucknall ships were made available as required. This joint service, known as Strick and Bucknall Line (later Strick and Ellerman Line), lasted for seventy years, although there was never any other connection between the two firms. During 1905, the Anglo-Arabian and Persian Steamship Co. Ltd. was merged with the Anglo-Algerian Steamship Co. (1896) Ltd. In addition another new company, La Commerciale Steam Navigation Co. Ltd. was formed by Mr. Strick and his friends in Paris. This company then was merged in 1913 with the Anglo-Algerian Steamship Co. (1896) Ltd. to form Strick Line Ltd.

Over the years, as trade expanded, the Gulf run took on more and more ports, loading at South Wales, London, Manchester, Glasgow, Antwerp and Marseilles for discharge at Port Sudan, Djibouti, Aden, Muscat and sundry small Arabian and Persian ports with the terminus still at Basrah, but there was no fixed service, vessels sailing in a haphazard manner as and when possible.

In 1909, at the request of the Board of Trade, it was agreed to operate a twice monthly service outwards and a monthly service homewards so that, seventeen years after the first tentative voyage to the Gulf, Stricks had a liner service and they also had ships which befitted that status, many being fast for their day, with accommodation for up to twenty passengers, lounge, music room, dining saloon and stewardesses. Tweendecks were also fitted for carrying pilgrims for Mecca to the adjacent port of Jeddah.

Also in 1909, Frank C. Strick & Co. Ltd., in association with M. Mesnier's firm of Soc. Commerciale d'Affretements et de Commission, formed another new company, La Tunisienne Steam Navigation Co. Ltd., to operate in the Mediterranean trade and began to build a fleet of ships especially for the carriage of coal and iron ore with names of localities in North Africa ending in 'A'. The Mokta Company was involved in the financing of some of the ships and this led to one of them being named MOKTA.These ships had a different livery to the Gulf fleet, which included a funnel device of Stricks red, white and blue, with the letter 'M' in the centre for Mesnier. This company was managed, as were all the others, by Frank C. Strick & Co. Ltd. but from this time on the Gulf fleet and Mediterranean fleet were entirely separate, with no inter-changing of vessels, nor, indeed, of personnel. There was now no need for the Gulf trade to be 'helped out' because of the Bucknall agreement.

At this point, mention should be made of various activities and developments in the Gulf. In 1901, William Knox D'Arcy, an Australian, obtained a concession from the Shah of Persia to explore for oil and commenced drilling in 1903. He first struck oil in commercial quantities at Masjid-e-Suleiman, in the Zagros mountains, on 26th May 1908. During this period, ships of the Anglo-Algerian Steamship Co. (1896) Ltd. carried large quantities of equipment, stores, and personnel to the Gulf for the D'Arcy exploration teams and, together with the Strick agents in the area, had rendered great assistance to them. In 1909, the Anglo-Persian Oil Company Limited, later Anglo-Iranian Oil Company Limited, and now British Petroleum Co. Ltd., was formed and took over the concession from D'Arcy.

By 1910, with the expansion of his various Gulf interests, Mr. Strick thought it vital to have his own offices at the main ports and trading centres, and in January 1911 he entered into partnership with Lloyd, Scott & Co. Ltd. to form Strick, Scott & Co. Ltd. with offices at Basrah, Mohammerah, Ahwaz and Baghdad. This company also formed a close association with R. G. Shaw & Co., an old established firm of East India merchants, and it was R. G. Shaw & Co. who operated the merchanting and management side of the Strick, Scott business.

Various export commodities were purchased for shipment and subsequent sale in the U.K., Continent and U.S.A. Cargoes of red oxide from Hormuz Island and dates from Basrah were typical of the goods carried in quantity for very many years, the date trade being managed by the Iraq Produce Co., a 100% subsidiary of Strick, Scott. Other shipments included barley, carpets, sheepskins, mother of pearl shells, gum arabic, wild almonds, oak barrel staves, cotton and cotton seed. Oil company and commercial equipment returning to U.K. for servicing etc. was also carried. The company acted as merchants for a number of U.K. companies, distributing their products throughout the area.

Because of the strong business ties that had been formed between the Anglo-Persian Oil Co. Ltd. and Stricks, in 1911 the oil company appointed Strick, Scott as their managing agents and their managing director, Mr. Charles Greenway, was appointed to the Strick, Scott board. Mr. Greenway also became a director of the Anglo-Algerian Steamship Co. (1896) Ltd. Strick, Scott acted as agents in the Gulf for the oil company until the early 1920's by which time the oil business had grown to such an extent that they decided to open their own office at Abadan and dispense with agents. Most of the Strick, Scott staff who had been engaged in oil company work were transferred to this new office.

By the end of 1912, the La Tunisienne Steam Navigation Co. Ltd. had four ships in service and a fifth on the stocks and was now in a position to maintain the Mediterranean service. This meant that the ships of Anglo-Algerian Steamship Co. (1896) Ltd. were employed solely in the Gulf trade and the name had become outdated and inappropriate. On 1st January 1913 the Anglo-Algerian Steamship Co. (1896) Ltd. and the La Commerciale Steam Navigation Co. Ltd. were merged under the new name of Strick Line Ltd. This company also had M. Jules Mesnier as it's first chairman.

At the commencement of the 1914-18 war, the liner service to the Gulf was suspended and from then until July 1915 only three vessels made the voyage from the U.K. to the Gulf. Turkey, which at that time ruled the area now known as Iraq, was undecided as to which side to ally herself, and consequently Strick Line was unable to trade to Basrah. Sailings from Manchester and Marseilles were suspended and vessels maintained only an infrequent service to the lower Gulf ports and Bushire. When Turkey finally decided to align herself with Germany our oil supplies were threatened, so Britain sent an army of occupation to what was then known as Mesopotamia. At this point a rather ironical incident occurred. In an attempt to hamper the advance of the British troops, the Germans scuttled a ship in the Shatt-el-Arab river to block the channel. This ship was the EKBATANA which had started life in 1905 as the TURKISTAN and was sold to a German firm in 1910 and so a ship which was built to provide a service to Basrah was now used in an attempt to block it.

From July 1915 a reduced service was maintained throughout the remainder of the war but most of the ships were requisitioned at one time or another. Losses were heavy, but Stricks were kept busy as they also managed eight captured enemy vessels for the Government. Five of these enemy vessels were purchased from the Government, two during the war and three later, and one of these, purchased in 1921, was another vessel built for Strick and sold to Germans. She was another TURKISTAN built in 1911, but she could not take her original name as this had been given to one of the war built ships, so she became the SHAHRISTAN and was to become the 'name' ship of another new company a year later.

In 1919 with the fleet sorely depleted, the cost of replacements greatly increased and Mr. Strick in his seventieth year negotiations were commenced which were to lead to the sale of the remaining Strick Line fleet and business. The new owner of Strick Line Ltd. was Gray, Daws and Company which was controlled by Lord Inchcape, Chairman of the P&O Steam Navigation Company. The sale related only to Strick Line Ltd. and did not include Frank C. Strick and Co. Ltd. or any of its other subsidiary companies.

After the sale of Strick Line Ltd. the various trades continued as before the war, except that the London & Paris Steamship Co. Ltd. had been left with no ships. In fact, it never owned another ship in it's own name, although the Company was to remain active as a holding company.

The La Tunisienne Steam Navigation Co. Ltd. continued to operate the U.K.-Mediterranean coal and iron ore trade under the management of Frank C. Strick and Co. Ltd. and the Gulf trade was continued with the few remaining ships, the fleet being slowly built up again under the joint management of Frank C. Strick and Co. Ltd. and Gray, Daws and Company.

During 1920 Mr. Strick formed a new company, the London, Paris and Marseilles Steamship Co. Ltd. with an authorised capital of one million pounds. In 1922 three new companies were formed to operate the Gulf fleet. These were the Serbistan Steamship Co. Ltd., the Shahristan Steamship Co. Ltd. and the Turkistan Steamship Co. Ltd., each having two ships.

In 1923 Strick Line Ltd. became Strick Line (1923) Ltd. and in May 1923 Gray, Daws and Company offered to sell the Company to the P&O Steam Navigation Company. It was however decided that The Hain Steamship Co. Ltd., a subsidiary of P&O Steam Navigation Company, should purchase the whole of the share capital of Strick Line (1923) Ltd., the Shahristan Steamship Co. Ltd., the Serbistan Steamship Co. Ltd. and the Turkistan Steamship Co. Ltd. for £573,468.

A number of other changes took place in 1923. The London office of Frank C. Strick and Co. Ltd. was moved into the P&O building at 117/121 Leadenhall Street and all new ships were registered at London. Also in 1923 Strick, Scott and Co. Ltd. went into liquidation and Frank C. Strick and Co. (Busra) Ltd. was formed in it's place. This company continued to serve the Gulf fleet and also took over the large import/export business built up by Strick, Scott and Co. Ltd. at Basrah and other ports. They also had a fleet of barges, lighters and tugs on the river.

Meanwhile, Mr. Strick, although now an old man, continued his wide business interests and even continued to expand them. His old friend and associate M. J. Mesnier died in Paris and his place as chairman of Soc. Commerciale d'Affretements et de Commission was taken by another old friend and associate, M. Felix Gorche, who had also been a founder director of London & Paris Steamship Co. Ltd. In 1921, whilst re-organising the Cardiff office, Mr. Strick and Mr. Gorchs formed a new company, Strick, Gorchs & Co. Ltd., both holding a 50% interest. This brought still closer the ties between the British and French companies, who already had a joint interest in La Tuñisienne Steam Navigation Co. Ltd. and the coal export trade. This was continued until 1945 when F. C. Strick & Co. (S. Wales) Ltd. took up most of the French shares.

In 1922, Mr. Strick bought a secondhand American vessel, the WEST CARUTH from the U.S. Shipping Board, and formed a new company, The North Devon Steamship Co. Ltd. to operate her. This was completely unconnected with all his other companies, and she carried a livery of her own, with a white 'S' on a blue band on a black funnel. He renamed the ship EXMOOR and although he only kept her for a little over a year, the company remained in existence until 1942 when it was renamed Frank C. Strick & Co (S. Wales) Ltd., operating in conjunction with Strick, Gorchs Ltd.

In 1925, the Gulf fleet went over to Indian crews recruited in Bombay. When the Gulf trade was first started the ships had European sailors and stewards, with Arab firemen, but after a while went over to all European crew until 1920 when Chinese catering staff were employed. From 1925 the sailors and firemen were Indian, the catering staff were christians from Goa, whilst the carpenters were Chinese, at first from Bombay but later, after Indian independence, from Hong Kong.

Ships continued to be built at regular intervals for both Strick Line (1923) Ltd. and La Tunisienne Steam Navigation Co. Ltd. but 1927 saw the last of a long line of ships from the William Gray yard at West Hartlepool, this being the ARABISTAN for Strick Line (1923) Ltd. The yard had built most of the Strick ships since the BALUCHISTAN of 1896.

A new connection was made in 1926 when the first of another long line was launched by John Readhead & Sons Ltd. at South Shields. This was the ARABISTAN but the vessel never sailed for Strick Line as she was sold before completion. From this time on Readheads built almost all Strick ships.

During the 1920's and 30's the Gulf service operated two vessels per month from London and one from Glasgow and Manchester. Regular sailings were also made from South Wales, Middlesbrough, Amsterdam, Antwerp and Marseilles. Ports of discharge in the Gulf had increased to more than a dozen.

By 1928, approaching the age of eighty but still very active in business, Mr. Strick decided to re-acquire an interest in the Gulf trade and Strick Line (1923) Ltd. He was able to negotiate with Lord Inchcape for the purchase of a 49% interest in Strick Line (1923) Ltd. and the Shahristan Steamship Co. Ltd. by the London & Paris Steamship Co. Ltd. for £236,228 and so once again he had a share in all sides of the business although he would never again have control of the Gulf trade.

The Turkistan Steamship Co. Ltd. and the Serbistan Steamship Co. Ltd. were liquidated and The Hain Steamship Co. Ltd. retained the controlling share in Strick Line (1923) Ltd. and the Shahristan Steamship Co. Ltd. on behalf of the P&O Steam Navigation Company. In 1935 the P&O Steam Navigation Company took over this controlling share from The Hain Steamship Co. Ltd. for £210,000.

Also in 1928 another new company was formed. This was in association with William Cory & Sons Ltd., long established in the coal shipping business. The company was named Cory & Strick (Steamers) Ltd. and had six ships built between 1928 and 1931, all with names similar to those of La Tunisienne Steam Navigation Co. Ltd. which they joined in the coal and iron ore trade from the U.K. to the Mediterranean. Their livery was similar to that of the La Tunisienne Steam Navigation Co. Ltd., except that the well known Cory black diamond replaced the Mesnier 'M' on white diamond on the funnel.

In 1930 the group formed it's own ship chandlery business to supply ships with stores and equipment direct from the manufacturers. This company was named United Ship Supplies Ltd.

In 1931 the group was caught up in the depression in world trade, and soon quite a few of the Gulf ships and most of the Mediterranean ships were laid up in various rivers and ports where they stayed for some years. No new ships were built until 1937 when trade started to recover and, indeed, no ship was ever again built for the coal and iron ore trade, although two second-hand ships were purchased as replacements after World War II. Building for the Gulf trade commenced again in 1937, but the peaceful trade now resuming was not to last for long.

In 1939, Mr. Strick semi-retired from business and only travelled to London from his country home at Streatley-on-Thames, about once a week, just to keep in touch with the activities of his many companies and to meet colleagues and friends of the shipping world. He was then in his ninetieth year and had owned ships for fifty two years.

At the commencement of hostilities, the three fleets comprised a total of 25 vessels, of approximately 207,000 tons deadweight being Strick Line (1923) Ltd. 12, Shahristan Steamship Co. Ltd. 1,La Tunisienne Steam Navigation Co. Ltd. 6, and Cory & Strick (Steamers) Ltd. 6. Between 1939 and 1945 Strick Line built 8 vessels, including two of company design ordered prior to the war from Readheads, the others being Government standard vessels. Five of the standard ships were motor vessels and were the first of this type owned by the company. Frank C. Strick & Co. Ltd. also managed several vessels for the Government at various times and by the end of the war twenty owned or managed vessels had been lost. Aboard these ships were a total of 1,075 crew and 89 passengers, of which 335 lost their lives. The number of honours awarded to seagoing personnel serving in the fleets was 27, being 6 O.B.E., 6 M.B.E., 1 B.E.M. and 14 Commendations.

By 1943 Cory & Strick (Steamers) Ltd. had lost three of their six ships and the remaining vessels were disposed of, two being sold and one transferred to La Tunisienne Steam Navigation Co. Ltd. Thus the Cory & Strick association came to an end after fifteen years.

In January 1943, the founder and chairman of Frank C. Strick & Co. Ltd., Mr. F. C. Strick, died, in his 94th year. He had controlled his own many businesses for 58 years and his name was well known throughout the world.

Towards the end of the war, Strick Line commenced using Liverpool as a regular loading port, appointing Messrs. Japp, Hatch and later Messrs. Edward Turner & Co. as agents.

Strick Line ships served in all theatres of the war and apart from losses there were many close calls and many deeds of heroism and daring. The fleet was represented at the evacuations of France and Crete, and various landings, and many hazardous cargoes were carried through very dangerous waters. Four ships spent many months towards the end of the war in the Far East, remaining on Government service long after the war was over. The KOHISTAN for instance did not arrive back home from this service until August 1946, almost a year after the Japanese surrender.

Another name change came in 1946 when Strick Line (1923) Ltd. reverted to the old style of 1913 and became Strick Line Ltd. once more. In 1947 with building restrictions relaxed, and owners being allowed to build ships to their own design again, Stricks went to Readheads for their new building programme. Between March 1947 and October 1950, Strick Line Ltd. took delivery of eight new vessels and La Tunisienne Steam Navigation Co. Ltd. purchased two secondhand ships.

In 1951 the Iranian Government suddenly cancelled the oil concessions and nationalised the Anglo-Iranian Oil Co. Ltd. This considerably affected the Strick Line and it's trade to Iran, as all shipments of stores and materials to the former oil company ceased until 1953 when an international consortium was formed to operate the exploration and production of oil for the Iranian Government and trade revived again. In the meantime the State of Kuwait started to exploit it's oil reserves and commenced a wide development programme which gave trade between the U.K. and Kuwait a great boost. As more and more oil reserves were found and developed in various other parts of the Gulf, Strick and Ellerman Lines increased their trade and also the number of ports served.

Early in the 1950's, the coal exporting trade began to decline and it was decided to sell the ships of the La Tunisienne Steam Navigation Co. Ltd. and close down the business. The last of that company's vessels was sold in 1951 and so ended over 60 years in the coal and iron ore trade.

BALTISTAN *W.S.P.L.*

The year 1953 saw a major change in shipbuilding policy when, in July, John Readhead & Sons Ltd. delivered the BALTISTAN. She was the first motor vessel designed and built for the company and from that time no more steamers were built.

The company's head office made another move in 1956, as the old P&O building in Leadenhall Street was about to be demolished. The new home was in Ellerman's new building in Camomile Street where United Ship Supplies Ltd. also moved into an office.

During October 1956 the nationalisation of the Suez Canal took place and the subsequent landing by British and French troops. The Egyptians sank a number of ships to block the canal and for the next four months the company's ships had to make the long haul around the Cape of Good Hope to the Gulf, usually calling at Durban to refuel.

February 1958 brought the greatest peacetime disaster in the history of the Company when the SEISTAN, on only her second voyage, blew up in Bahrain harbour, killing 58 people including the Master, Captain W. A. Chappell. She had on board a consignment of seismic explosives, fuses and detonators.

SEISTAN *W.S.P.L.*

In 1959, Strick Line Ltd. and the Shahristan Steamship Co. Ltd. owned twenty-five ships, but about this time the effects of increased competition began to be felt, combined with a reduction in trade from the U.K. as the developing countries around the Gulf increasingly purchased their requirements from worldwide sources. The company began to dispose of all old and uneconomical vessels. Between 1959 and 1963 all the pre-war and wartime built ships were sold, either to breakers or for further use, a total of eleven ships in all, whilst new ships continued to be built at an average of one per year, so that by 1963 the combined fleets numbered seventeen vessels, all built since 1947.

Early in 1961 it was decided that the practice of having shipping companies managed by independently owned management companies was outdated and negotiations were begun in May for Strick Line Ltd. to acquire all the shares in Frank C. Strick & Co. Ltd. This purchase duly took place in Octobrer 1962 and from that date on Frank C. Strick & Co. Ltd. became a wholly owned subsidiary of Strick Line Ltd. although retaining the sole management of Strick Line Ltd. and the Shahristan Steamship Co. Ltd. This meant that for the first time P&O had a controlling interest of 51% in all the company's operations.

In 1962, due to changes in the laws relating to foreign companies working in Iraq, and the decreasing trade to both Iraq and Iran, the Baghdad and Basrah offices of Frank C. Strick & Co. (Busreh) Ltd. were closed. The agency business was taken over by Busreh Slipway Company, a subsidiary of Gray, Mackenzie & Co. Ltd. and the reduced trading business was continued by R. G. Shaw & Co., whilst Gray, Mackenzie were appointed Strick agents throughout Iran. In 1966 the Liverpool office of Frank C. Strick & Co. Ltd. was opened and took over the agency work previously carried out by Messrs Edward Turner & Co.

Once again the Suez Canal was closed to shipping on the outbreak of the Arab-Israeli six days war of June 1967 and the long trip around the Cape became necessary for the second time since the war years. To maintain the schedules and keep the service up to the usual standard, a great deal of re-routing was needed and a number of additional ships were taken on charter. The distance from the U.K. to the Gulf was now over 11,000 miles but, as usual, the company quickly and efficiently adapted, and settled down to a situation which was to continue for the rest of it's existence.

In 1969 the Iraqi Government nationalised their shipping industry and the Strick Agency was taken over by the Iraqi Maritime Transport Co. with offices at Basrah and Baghdad.

During 1971 P&O formed the General Cargo Division and began transferring ships to it from the various fleets in the group, as part of a rationalisation policy. Negotiations were started for the purchase of the minority shareholding in Strick Line Ltd. and the Shahristan Steamship Co. Ltd. and these were completed in March 1972 when the 49% which Mr. Strick had negotiated for in 1928 was acquired again by P&O. This time the transaction also involved the company which he had formed in 1885, namely Frank C. Strick & Co. Ltd.

The fleet in March 1972 consisted of seventeen vessels, but one of these, the TANGISTAN, the oldest ship in the fleet, was already on her way to the breakers. She was the last steamer in the fleet. Four ships were immediately transferred to the General Cargo Division whilst the next oldest ship, the BALTISTAN was sold. In 1973, two more of the oldest ships were sold and on 19th April of that year all the remaining ships with the exception of the NIGARISTAN were transferred to the General Cargo Divsion. On 14th February 1974 the last remaining Strick Line vessel, the NIGARISTAN, was transferred to the General Cargo Division of P&O and the name of Strick went out of the register.

In the first few months of 1975 all the remaining thirteen ships were given P&O names, commencing with 'STRATH' in line with other ships of the General Cargo Division and the famous 'STANS' were no more. From 1977 these remaining ships were sold off in rapid succession, and by early 1979 only the STRATHAIRD, formerly the NIGARISTAN, remained as sole survivor under the British flag of a once great fleet whose flag and funnel had been instantly recognised all over the world and whose record and reputation was second to none.

FLEET LIST NOTES

On first sight, especially after reading the history of the Company, the Strick fleets look complicated and involved. In some respects this is true, but in fact the fleets fall naturally into three main groups, and the fleet lists which follow have been laid out in such a way as to reflect these groupings.

The first group consists of the fleets which operated the trades from the United Kingdom to both the Mediterranean and the Persian Gulf from 1889 until 1912. These ships were more or less interchangeable on the routes and were owned as follows:

Anglo-Algerian Steamship Co. Ltd.
Anglo-Arabian and Persian Steamship Co. Ltd.
La Commerciale Steam Navigation Co. Ltd.

To these has been added The Dwina Ltd., which only operated in the Gulf.

The second group are the Companies which operated only on the U.K. to Persian Gulf trade, from 1913 until 1972. These were:

Strick Line Ltd.
Serbistan Steamship Co. Ltd.
Shahristan Steamship Co. Ltd.
Turkistan Steamship Co. Ltd.
Strick Line (1923) Ltd. (This became Strick Line Ltd. in 1946).

The third group are the fleets which operated only on the coal and iron ore trades between U.K./Continent and Mediterranean. These were:

London & Paris Steamship Co. Ltd.
La Tunisienne Steam Navigation Co. Ltd.
Cory & Strick (Steamers) Ltd.

To these has been added Mr. Strick's own North Devon Steamship Co. Ltd.

Before any of these, has been placed a group of ships under the heading Frank C. Strick & Co. This was not a fleet as such. The ships under this heading were mainly those which were ordered but sold before or during construction, or upon completion. There were, however, just a few other ships which Messrs. F. C. Strick & Co. retained under their ownership.

Finally, there comes the list of ships which were managed for the Government or other Owners.

The notation I and II, etc., in brackets after a ship's name indicates that she is the first, second, etc., ship of that name in the fleet. The dates following the name are those of entering and leaving the fleet or coming under and leaving the management of the Company.

On the first line is given the ship's Official Number (O.N.) in the British Registry, followed by her tonnages gross ('g') and net ('n'). dimensions given are registered length × beam × depth in feet and tenths except for ship number H.8 and K.36 to K.50 where the overall length × beam × draught at summer deadweight are given.

On the second line is give the type of engines and the name of the engine builders 'C.2-cyl.' denotes compound two cylinder steam engines, 'T.3-cyl,' = triple expansion three cylinder steam engines, 'Q.4-cy.' = quadruple expansion four cylinder steam engines and for motor vessels the number of cylinders is given and whether they are two stroke cycle (2 S.C.) or four stroke cycle (4 S.C.) single acting (S.A.).

F. C. STRICK AND CO.

A.1 NORMAND (1887-1888)
ON. 89123. 1,238g, 786n. 235.0 × 31.9 × 17.8 feet.
C2-cyl. by Blair and Co. Ltd., Stockton on Tees.
12.1877: Launched by Robert Irvine and Co., West Hartlepool (Yard No. 23) as NORMAND for J. Mesnier, France. *1887:* Purchased by Frank C. Strick. *1888:* Sold to T.S. Blues and Co., South Shields. *28.2.1897:* Sailed from Newport, Mon. on a voyage to Bilbao with a cargo of coal and disappeared.

A.2 DWINA (1895-1905)
ON. 44835. 983g, 795n. 233.2 × 28.9 × 14.9 feet.
C2-cyl. by the shipbuilder.
3.1862: Launched by C. and W. Earle, Hull (Yard No. 69) as DWINA for C. M. Norwood and Co., London. *22.6.1895:* Purchased by F. C. Strick and Co. *1905:* Transferred to The Dwina Ltd. *24.11.1909:* Abandoned after breaking her moorings and sinking in deep water whilst partially submerged to act as a landing stage at Baraim Island in the Shatt el Arab.

A.3 HERONSPOOL (1898)
See SHAHRISTAN(I) (No. B.8).

A.4 NEWBUILDING No. 811
5,106g, 3,205n. 400.0 × 53.5 × 27.1 feet.
T3-cyl. by Central Marine Engine Works, West Hartlepool.
27.9.1912: Launched and *11.1912* completed by Wm. Gray and Co. Ltd., West Hartlepool (Yard No. 811) as ARAKAN for Rotterdamsche Lloyd (W. Ruys & Zonen managers), The Netherlands. *16.11.1912:* Ran trials. The vessel had been ordered by F. C. Strick and Co. Ltd. who sold the contract before construction commenced. *1924:* Sold to Lyle Shipping Co. Ltd., Glasgow for £40,000 and renamed CAPE COMORIN. *1934:* Sold to Italian shipbreakers for £6,950 and *19.12.1934* arrived at Venice to be broken up.

A.5 NEWBUILDING No. 816
6,070g, 3,895n. 400.0 × 53.5 × 34.6 feet.
T3-cyl. by Central Marine Engine Works, West Hartlepool.
7.11.1912: Launched and *2.1913* completed by Wm. Gray and Co. Ltd., West Hartlepool (Yard No. 816) as BOETON for Stoomvaart Maats. Nederland., The Netherlands. *24.2.1913:* Ran trials. The vessel had been ordered by F. C. Strick and Co. Ltd. who sold the contract before construction commenced. *1.4.1927:* Sold to N. V. Java — China — Japan Lijn, The Netherlands and renamed TJIMENTENG. *1932:* Sold to Japanese shipbreakers but resold to Russian owners for further trading and renamed POSTYSHEV. *11.5.1933:* Wrecked near Horomushiro Island.

BATJAN W.S.P.L.

A.6 NEWBUILDING No. 819

6,286g, 4,051n. 400.0 × 53.5 × 34.6 feet.
T3-cyl. by Central Marine Engine Works, West Hartlepool.
23.12.1912: Launched and *3.1913* completed by Wm. Gray and Co Ltd., West Hartlepool (Yard No. 819) as BATJAN for Stoomvaart Maats. Nederland., The Netherlands. *15.3.1913:* Ran trials. The vessel had been ordered by F. C. Strick and Co. Ltd. who sold the contract before construction commenced. *3.1918:* Taken over at New York by the United States Shipping Board (Emergency Fleet Corporation), U.S.A. *8.6.1919:* Returned to owners at Amsterdam. *22.2.1927:* Sold to N. V. Java – China – Japan Lijn, The Netherlands and renamed TJIKAMPEK. *1932:* Sold to Japanese shipbreakers.

NOORDERDYK W.S.P.L.

A.7 NEWBUILDING No. 820
7,156g, 4,598n. 420.0 × 54.5 × 36.2 feet.
T3-cyl. by Central Marine Engine Works, West Hartlepool.
21.2.1913: Launched and *5.1913* completed by Wm. Gray and Co. Ltd., West Hartlepool (Yard No. 820) as NOORDERDYK for Holland Amerika Lijn, The Netherlands. *10.5.1913:* Ran trials. The vessel had been ordered by F. C. Strick and Co. Ltd. who sold the contract before construction commenced. *22.2.1917:* Torpedoed and sunk 30 miles West of Bishop Rock by the German submarine U.21 whilst on a voyage from New York to Rotterdam via Falmouth with grain.

A.8 SHAHRISTAN (IV) (1913)
ON. 133114. 4,791g, 3,038n. 380.0 × 51.5 × 27.5 feet.
T3-cyl. by Central Marine Engine Works, West Hartlepool.
10.2.1913: Launched by Wm. Gray and Co. Ltd., West Hartlepool (Yard No. 822) for F. C. Strick and Co. Ltd. and *4.1913* completed as OZARDA for British India Steam Navigation Co. Ltd., Glasgow. *12.1938:* Sold to shipbreakers for £9100.

Contract price £62,000 including machinery. Payable £5000 when keel laid, £6000 when framed, £6000 when plated, £3000 when launched and the balance of £42,000 on completion. The builders to allow the purchasers 4% per annum interest on instalments prior to completion. On 25.2.1913 *the owners wrote to the builders referring to. . . . . "our contract with the British India Company provides for their taking delivery of the steamer on completion of a satisfactory trial trip. Consequently we shall complete our contract with your goodselves but any extras and alterations the British India Company may arrange with you to make must be a matter of settlement between you and them."*

SHAHRISTAN as **OZARDA** *W.S.P.L.*

A.9 SHAHRISTAN (V) (1913)
ON. 136261. 4783g, 2997n. 380.0 × 51.5 × 27.5 feet.
T3-cyl. by Central Marine Engine Works, West Hartlepool.
15.9.1913: Launched by Wm. Gray and Co. Ltd., West Hartlepool (Yard No. 830) for F.C. Strick and Co. Ltd. and *11.1913* completed as ORNA for British India Steam Navigation Co. Ltd., Glasgow. *1933:* Sold to Japanese shipbreakers for £6650 with delivery at Osaka.

Contract price £63,750 including £17,900 for machinery. Payable £5000 when keel laid, £6000 when framed, £6000 when plated, £3000 when launched, £3750 on delivery and the balance of £40,000 payable over 4 years in equal ½ yearly instalments plus interest at 5% per annum in advance. The builders to allow interest at 4% per annum on instalments paid up to completion.

SHAHRISTAN as **ORNA** *W.S.P.L.*

A.10 HUNTSTRICK (1915-1917)
ON. 115342. 8151g, 5284n. 501.0 × 59.3 × 32.9 feet.
Two T3-cyl. by the shipbuilder.
30.10.1902: Launched and *12.1902* completed by Workman, Clark and Co. Ltd., Belfast (Yard No. 193) as IRAK for Irak Steam Ship Co. Ltd. (J. H. Welsford and Co., managers), Liverpool. *1911:* Sold to T. and J. Brocklebank Ltd., Liverpool and renamed MANDASOR. *1913:* Sold to Hamburg — Amerikanische Packetfahrt Actien Gesellschaft, Germany and renamed BELGIA. *5.8.1914:* Arrived at Newport, Mon. from Boston. Condemned as a prize and requisitioned by the Admiralty. *1915:* Purchased by F. C. Strick and Co. Ltd., and renamed HUNTSTRICK. *8.6.1917:* Torpedoed and sunk 80 miles W.N.W. of Cape Spartel by the German submarine U.39. The master and fourteen members of the crew were lost. The vessel was on a voyage from London to Salonica with government stores and troops.

HUNTSTRICK as **IRAK** *W.S.P.L.*

A.11 ROOKE (1917-1921)

ON. 140304. 3391g, 2194n. 345.9 × 48.1 × 23.0 feet.
T3-cyl. by North Eastern Marine Engineering Co. Ltd., Sunderland.
5.11.1907: Launched and *1.1908* completed by Chantiers Navals Anversois S.A., Hoboken, Belgium (Yard No. 35) as SLAWENTZITZ for Seetransport G.m.b.H. (R. Loesener, manager), Germany. *1909:* Sold to Rhederei — Vereinigung G.m.b.H., Germany. *8.9.1914:* Captured North East of the Azores by H.M.S. VINDICTIVE whilst waiting to supply the German auxiliary cruiser KAISER WILHELM DER GROSSE. *14.9.1914:* Arrived at Gibraltar and condemned as a prize. *1915:* Requisitioned by the British Government, placed under the management of Elder, Dempster and Co., Liverpool, and renamed ROOKE. *1916:* Sold to Tyzack and Branfoot, Newcastle. *1917:* Purchased by F.C. Strick and Co. Ltd., *1921:* Sold to E. E. Hadjilias, Greece and renamed THETIS. *1929:* Sold to L. Vlachakis, Greece and renamed FANEROMENI. *1940:* Sold to N. Th. Bulgaris, Greece. *23.10.1943:* Torpedoed and sunk in a position 16.21 S, 40.04 E. in the Mozambique Channel by the Japanese submarine I.37 whilst on a voyage from Mombasa for Durban with a cargo of soda and rubber. One crew member was lost.

A.12 NEWBUILDING No. 888

ON. 139625. 4460g, 2818n. 380.3 × 52.0 × 26.0 feet.
T3-cyl. by Central Marine Engine Works, West Hartlepool.
7.1917: Launched and *11.1917* completed by Wm. Gray and Co. Ltd., West Hartlepool (Yard No. 888) as ANGLESEA for Cardigan Steam Ship Co. Ltd., (Jenkins Bros., managers), Cardiff. The vessel had been ordered by F. C. Strick and Co. Ltd., who sold the contract before construction commenced. *1920:* J. Jenkins, Sons and Co. Ltd., appointed managers. *1921:* Transferred to Anglesea Steam Ship Co. Ltd., (same managers), Cardiff. *1922:* Sold to Portfield Steam Ship Co. Ltd., (W. E. Hinde and Co., managers), Cardiff and renamed PORTGWARRA. *1932:* Sold to New Era Steam Ship Co. Ltd., (Frank S. Dawson Ltd., managers), Cardiff and renamed THOMAS WALTON. *1937:* Transferred to Coronation Steam Ship Co. Ltd., (same managers), Cardiff. *7.12.1939:* Torpedoed and sunk East of Iceland in a position 67.52 N, 14.28 E. by the German submarine U.38 whilst on a voyage from Port Talbot for Narvik in ballast. Thirteen crew were lost.

ANGLESEA *Author's Collection*

A.13 KARA (II) (1919-1920).
ON. 136156. 2479g, 1473n. 303.0 × 43.0 × 20.9 feet.
T3-cyl. by Central Marine Engine Works, West Hartlepool.
30.7.1919: Launched and *10.1919* completed by Wm. Gray and Co. (1918) Ltd., West Hartlepool (Yard No. 926) for F.C. Strick and Co. Ltd. *11.10.1919:* Ran trials. *22.3.1920:* Wrecked at Cape Quintres, near Santander whilst on a voyage from Heysham to Bilbao in ballast.

The contract had been placed by The Shipping Controller at a cost based on materials and labour, plus profit and establishment charges of £14,500, and for instalment calculations this was deemed to total £68,500. Payable 20% when keel laid, 20% when framed, 20% when plated, 20% when launched and safely berthed and 20% on delivery.

A.14 NEWBUILDING No. 943
8439g, 5348n. 433.0 × 57.4 × 38.4 feet.
Two steam turbines by Central Marine Engine Works, West Hartlepool, double reduction geared to a single shaft.
21.4.1921: Launched and *10.1921* completed by Wm. Gray and Co. (1918) Ltd., Sunderland (Yard No. 943) as SIANTAR for Rotterdamsche Lloyd (W. Ruys & Zonen, managers), The Netherlands. The vessel had been ordered by F. C. Strick and Co. Ltd., who sold the contract before construction commenced. *2.3.1942:* Torpedoed, shelled and sunk by the Japanese submarine I.1 in the Indian Ocean in a position 21.20 S, 108.45 E. with the loss of 21 members of the crew. The vessel was on a voyage from Java to Fremantle.

SIANTAR *A. Duncan*

A.15 NEWBUILDING No. 948
8381g, 5343n. 433.0 × 57.4 × 38.4 feet.
Two steam turbines by Central Marine Engine Works, West Hartlepool, double reduction geared to a single shaft.
27.2.1922: Launched and *7.1922* completed by Wm. Gray and Co. (1918) Ltd., Sunderland (Yard No. 948) as MODJOKERTO for Rotterdamsche Lloyd (W. Ruys & Zonen, managers), The Netherlands. The vessel had been ordered by F. C. Strick and Co. Ltd., who sold the contract before construction commenced. *1.3.1942:* Attacked by the Japanese heavy cruiser CHIKUMA about 250 miles S.W. of Tjilatjap and badly damaged. Torpedoed and sunk later in the day by the Japanese submarine I.154 with the loss of 42 of her crew. The vessel was on a voyage from New York for Padang, Singapore and Rangoon.

A.16 ARABISTAN (VI) (1926)
ON. 149746. 4862g, 2971n. 400.0 × 55.2 × 25.7 feet.
T3-cyl. by the shipbuilder.
7.10.1926: Launched by J. Readhead and Sons Ltd., South Shields (Yard No.482) for F.C. Strick and Co. Ltd., who had purchased the hull which was being built "on spec". Sold for £80,000 whilst fitting out to Turnbull Scott Shipping Co. Ltd. (Turnbull, Scott and Co., managers), London and *11.1926* completed as SOUTHGATE. *1946:* Sold to Skibs A/S Otteid (F. F. Zimmer, manager), Norway and renamed OTTEID. *1947:* Sold to N. A. Kydoniefs, Greece and renamed DIMITRIOS A. KYDONIEFS. *1960:* Sold to Hong Kong shipbreakers for £60,000 and *28.2.1960* arrived at Hong Kong to be broken up by Shin Wing Hong.

ANGLO-ALGERIAN STEAMSHIP CO. LTD.

ANGLO-ALGERIAN STEAMSHIP CO. (1896) LTD.

This Company was formed in 1889 to operate the steamer ALPHONSE PARRAN in the coal trade from South Wales ports to Northern France and later, with chartered tonnage, to Mediterranean ports, returning with iron ore. In 1896 the company went into voluntary liquidation and a new company was formed to replace it, named Anglo-Algerian Steamship Co. (1896) Ltd.

Ships of the company were employed in the Mediterranean coal and iron ore trade and also assisted in the Gulf trade. In 1905 the Anglo-Arabian and Persian Steamship Co. Ltd. was merged with it and thereafter it served both trades until 1910 when the La Tunisienne Steam Navigation Co. Ltd. was formed to operate the Mediterranean trade. On 1st January 1913 it merged with La Commerciale Steam Navigation Co. Ltd. to form Strick Line Ltd.

The livery included a black funnel with a broad white band on which were alternate red and blue chevrons, a black hull with white upperworks and buff masts and derricks. The actual date of adoption of this livery is uncertain but is thought to have been about 1893.

B.1 ALPHONSE PARRAN (1889-1897)
ON. 89125. 1876g, 1203n. 270.0 × 37.0 × 17.4 feet.
T3-cyl. by the shipbuilder.
1.7.1889: Launched and *8.1889* completed by Wm. Doxford and Sons, Sunderland (Yard No. 188) for Anglo-Algerian Steamship Co. Ltd. *1896:* Owners restyled as Anglo-Algerian Steamship Co. (1896) Ltd. *1897:* Sold to Joh. E. v. d. Ohe, Norway and renamed PARRAN. *1898:* Sold to Joh. E. v. d. Ohe & Lund, Norway. *1905:* Sold to Vonderohe & Lund, Norway. *1909:* Sold to J. Lund & Co., Norway. *5.1910:* Sold to Norwegian shipbreakers and broken up at Bergen.

B.2 BALUCHISTAN (I) (1896-1899)
ON. 104951. 2409g, 1529n. 290.0 × 42.1 × 17.4 feet.
T3-cyl. by Central Marine Engine Works, West Hartlepool.
31.12.1895: Launched and *2.1896* completed by Wm. Gray and Co. Ltd., West Hartlepool (Yard No. 510) for Anglo-Algerian Steamship Co. (1896) Ltd. *1899:* Sold to Cia. Nav. Bachi (Hijos de Astigarraga, manager), Spain and renamed TOM. *14.4.1917:* Torpedoed and sunk in the Bay of Biscay by the German submarine UC26 whilst on a voyage from Bilbao to Cardiff with a cargo of iron ore.

Contract price £22,850 including £5850 (less 2% for cash) for machinery. Payable in cash on completion or £17,850 in cash on delivery and the balance payable over 3 years in equal ½ yearly instalments plus interest at 5% per annum in advance. Security of £5000 to be held in 2nd debentures in the owning company.

B.3 LARISTAN (1896-1899)
ON. 104954. 2134g, 1360n. 290.0 × 42.2 × 19.2 feet.
T3-cyl. by Central Marine Engine Works, West Hartlepool.
5.11.1896: Launched and *12.1896* completed by Wm. Gray and Co. Ltd., West Hartlepool (Yard No.526) for Anglo-Algerian Steamship Co. (1896) Ltd. *22.10.1899:* Sank off the Goodwin Sands following a collision with the British steamer CRIMEA, 1708/89 whilst on a voyage from Bona to Rotterdam with a cargo of iron ore.

Contract price £22,750 including £5550 for machinery. Payment in cash on completion or ¼ in cash on delivery and the balance payable over 3 years in equal ½ yearly instalments plus interest at 5% per annum in advance. Security to be held in debentures in the owning company.

B.4 AFGHANISTAN (I) (1897-1904)
ON. 104956. 2753g, 1751n. 306.3 × 43.2 × 18.3 feet.
T3-cyl. by Central Marine Engine Works, West Hartlepool.
4.1.1897: Launched and *2.1897* completed by Wm. Gray and Co. Ltd., West Hartlepool (Yard No. 531) for Anglo-Algerian Steamship Co. (1896) Ltd. *22.1.1904:* Stranded 40 miles north of Suakim, in the Red Sea, whilst on a voyage from the River Clyde to Karachi and became a total loss.

Contract price £25,500 including £6550 for machinery. Payable in cash on completion or £8000 in cash on delivery and the balance payable over 6 years in equal ½ yearly instalments plus interest at 5% per annum in advance. Security to be held in debentures in the owning company. The vessel to be secured by a mortgage on the whole boat and the vessel to be transferred to the purchaser pro rata as payments are made.

B.5 KOORDISTAN (1898-1906)
ON. 104958. 2740g, 1729n. 306.0 × 43.0 × 18.2 feet.
T3-cyl. by Central Marine Engine Works, West Hartlepool.
24.11.1897: Launched and *3.1898* completed by Wm. Gray and Co. Ltd., West Hartlepool (Yard No. 548) for Anglo-Algerian Steamship Co. (1896) Ltd. *1906:* Sold to Delmas Frères, France and renamed MAROC. *14.4.1918:* Torpedoed and sunk 2 miles S.E. of the Longships by the German submarine UB57.

Contract price £28,250 including £7625 for machinery. Payable in cash on completion or ¼ in cash on delivery and the balance payable over 3 years in equal ½ yearly instalments plus interest at 5% per annum in advance. Security to be held in debentures in the owning company.

B.6 GOOLISTAN (1898-1904)
ON. 104960. 2756g, 1740n. 306.0 × 43.1 × 18.3 feet.
T3-cyl. by Central Marine Engine Works, West Hartlepool.
7.2.1898: Launched and *4.1898* completed by Wm. Gray and Co. Ltd., West Hartlepool (Yard No. 549) for Anglo-Algerian Steamship Co. (1896) Ltd. *10.9.1904:* Sank 170 miles from Lisbon following a collision with the British steamer INVENTOR, 2291/78 whilst on a voyage from Karachi to Plymouth with a cargo of wheat. The third mate and six members of the crew were drowned.

Contract price £28,250 including £7625 for machinery. Payable in cash on completion or ¼ in cash on delivery and the balance payable over 3 years in equal ½ yearly instalments plus interest at 5% per annum in advance. Security to be held in debentures in the owning company.

B.7 NIGARISTAN (I) (1898-1906)
ON. 108279. 2305g, 1499n. 300.0 × 43.0 × 20.4 feet.
T3-cyl. by W. Allan and Co. Ltd., Sunderland.
29.10.1897: Launched and *12.1897* completed by R. Craggs and Sons, Middlesbrough (Yard No. 138) as HARPERLEY for J. and C. Harrison, London *1898*: Sold to J.A. Salton and Co., London. *1898:* Purchased by Anglo-Algerian Steamship Co. (1896) Ltd. and renamed NIGARISTAN. *1906:* Transferred to La Commerciale Steam Navigation Co. Ltd. *1907:* Sold to W. Kunstmann, Germany and renamed BRITANNIA. *14.6.1920:* Surrendered to Great Britain as a prize and allocated to The Shipping Controller (J. and J. Denholm Ltd., managers). *10.1920:* Transferred to the Greek Government. *1921:* Renamed ATHINAE. *1923:* Sold to Pnevmaticos, Rethymnis & Yannaghas, Greece and renamed AKTI. *11.2.1927:* Stranded at Alexandria whilst on a voyage from Constantza to Alexandria with a cargo of timber and declared a constructive total loss. Subsequently refloated *2.3.1927* and sold to Italian shipbreakers.

B.8 SHAHRISTAN (I) (1898-1905)
ON. 106842. 2893g, 1860n. 310.0 × 42.9 × 19.2 feet.
T3-cyl. by G. Clark Ltd., Sunderland.
4.2.1897: Launched and *3.1897* completed by Wm. Pickersgill and Sons, Sunderland (Yard No. 112) as HERONSPOOL for Heronspool Steam Ship Co. Ltd. (Japp and Kirby managers), Liverpool. *8.1898:* Purchased by F. C. Strick and Co. who intended to rename her ARMANISTAN but the ship was not renamed. *16.12.1898:* Transferred to Anglo-Algerian Steamship Co. (1896) Ltd. and renamed SHAHRISTAN. *11.1905:* Sold to Heyne und Hessenmuller, Germany and renamed FLORIAN HEYNE. *1908:* Sold to August Bolten Wm. Miller's Nachfolger, Germany and renamed HAARDT. *1913:* Sold to N. Kirzis & Co., Greece and renamed NICOLAS KIRZIS. *1914:* Reverted to August Bolten Wm. Miller's Nachfolger, Germany without change of name. *1914:* Sold to Emder Reederei, Germany and renamed MARIE. *1918:* Sold to Vereinigte Bugsir und Frachtschiff Ges., Germany and renamed STOR. *1918:* Sold to August Cords, Germany. *31.10.1918:* Stranded on the southern tip of Smoan, Sweden and abandoned as a total loss.

B.9 BARDISTAN (I) (1899)
ON. 109645. 2013g, 1298n. 275.0 × 41.6 × 17.7 feet.
T3-cyl. by Central Marine Engine Works, West Hartlepool.
13.12.1898: Launched and *3.1899* completed by Wm. Gray and Co. Ltd., West Hartlepool (Yard No. 574) for Anglo-Algerian Steamship Co. (1896) Ltd. who originally intended to name the ship DAGHISTAN. *10.1899:* Sold to Acties. Hekla (Mail & Holby managers), Norway and renamed LYSAKER. *1915:* Sold to B. Stolt-Nielsen, Norway. *6.7.1915:* Mined and sunk in the White Sea whilst on a voyage from Blyth to Archangel with a cargo of coal. The mine had been laid by the German auxiliary minelayer METEOR.

Contract price £26,150 including £6300 for machinery. Payable in cash on completion or £8300 in cash on delivery and the balance payable over 3½ years in equal ½ yearly instalments plus interest at 5% per annum in advance. Security to be held in debentures in the owning company. The vessel to be secured by a mortgage on the whole boat and the same to be transferred to the purchasers pro rata as the payments are met each 6 months.

MURISTAN *W.S.P.L.*

B.10 MURISTAN (I) (1899-1913)
ON. 109644. 2724g, 1736n. 306.5 × 43.2 × 18.3 feet.
T3-cyl. by North Eastern Marine Engineering Co. Ltd., Newcastle.
27.12.1898: Launched and *3.1899* completed by Wood, Skinner and Co. Ltd., Newcastle (Yard No. 77) for Anglo-Algerian Steamship Co. (1896) Ltd., *1.1.1913:* Transferred to Strick Line Ltd. *1913:* Sold to Cia. Maritima del Nervion (Urquijo y Aldecoa managers), Spain and renamed MAR CASPIO. *16.2.1918:* Captured by the German submarine U.152 and sunk by gunfire in a position 29.10N, 22.37W. whilst on a voyage from Palamos to New York with a cargo of cork.

SERBISTAN *Author's Collection*

B.11 SERBISTAN (I) (1899-1906)
ON. 108155. 2934g, 1851n. 312.0 × 43.2 × 24.3 feet.
T3-cyl. by G. Clark Ltd., Sunderland.
5.11.1896: Launched and *12.1896* completed by S. P. Austin and Son, Sunderland (Yard No. 184) as HARPENDEN for J. and C. Harrison, London. 1898: Sold to J.A. Salton and Co., London. *1899:* Purchased by Anglo-Algerian Steamship Co. (1896) Ltd. and renamed SERBISTAN. *1906:* Transferred to La Commerciale Steam Navigation Co. Ltd. *1.1.1913:* Transferred to Strick Line Ltd. *11.11.1916:* Sailed from St. Nazaire bound for Cardiff with a cargo of war munitions. *14.11.1916:* Chased by a German submarine off Ushant and subsequently arrived at Brest. *16.11.1916:* Sailed from Brest in continuation of her voyage to Cardiff and disappeared with her crew of 24 men.

B.12 BALUCHISTAN (II) (1900-1913)
ON. 108238. 2746g, 1711n. 314.1 × 45.5 × 20.9 feet.
T3-cyl. by G. Clark Ltd., Sunderland.
1.6.1897: Launched and *7.1897* completed by S. P. Austin and Son Ltd., Sunderland (Yard No. 193) as HARMONIC for J. and C. Harrison, London. *1900:* Purchased by Anglo-Algerian Steamship Co. (1896) Ltd. and renamed BALUCHISTAN. *1.1.1913:* Transferred to Strick Line Ltd. *1913:* Sold to J. Christensen, Norway and renamed RITA WALLEM. *1913:* Sold to Minamimanshu Tetsudo Kabushiki Kaisha, Japan and renamed RINSHO MARU, later rendered as RYUSHO MARU. *1920:* Sold to Dairen Kisen Kabushiki Kaisha, Japan. *1923:* Sold to Dairen Sato Kuni Kisen Kabushiki Kaisha, Japan. *1933:* Sold to shipbreakers.

B.13 BARDISTAN (II) (1900-1905)
ON. 108250. 2599g, 1651n. 314.0 × 44.1 × 20.7 feet.
T3-cyl. by Central Marine Engine Works, West Hartlepool.
12.8.1897: Launched and *9.1897* completed by Wm. Gray and Co. Ltd., West Hartlepool (Yard No. 544) as SAINT HELEN for Smith and Scaramanga, London. *1900:* Purchased by Anglo-Algerian Steamship Co. (1896) Ltd. and renamed BARDISTAN. *1905:* Sold to S. S. Arcola Co. Ltd. (William Thomson and Co. managers), St. John N.B. and renamed ARCOLA. *9.7.1908:* Wrecked in Hay Cove, St. Paul's Island, C.B. whilst on a voyage from Preston to Miramichi in ballast.

Contract price £27,500 including £6800 for machinery. Payable in cash on completion or £7500 in cash on delivery and the balance payable over 5 years in equal ½ yearly instalments plus interest at 5% per annum in advance. Collateral security being 55/64ths. registered in the builders' name and no less than 33/64ths. until the whole money paid. If the vessel had been registered in the ownership of a limited liability company the builders agreed to invest £500 in the said company.

B.14 AVRISTAN (I) (1900-1911)
ON. 113761. 2899g, 1821n. 324.0 × 47.1 × 21.7 feet.
T3-cyl. by G. Clark Ltd., Sunderland.
6.11.1900: Launched and *12.1900* completed by Wm. Pickersgill and Sons, Sunderland (Yard No. 129) for Anglo-Algerian Steamship Co. (1896) Ltd. *1911:* Sold to L. N. Condylis, Greece and renamed CONDYLIS. *1915:* Sold to Akties Dampskibs. Finland (A. Jensen manager), Denmark and renamed FINLAND. *1915:* Sold to American Transportation Co. Inc., U.S.A. (a German controlled corporation) and renamed GENESEE. *19.11.1915:* Captured off St. Lucia whilst on a voyage from Norfolk, Va. to Montevideo and condemned as a prize. *6.3.1916:* Arrived at Hull and registered under the Government of St. Lucia. *1921:* Sold to S. N. Valmadis, Greece and renamed ELENI. *1929:* Sold to Rederi A/B Malin (A. Kristensen manager), Sweden for £12,500 and renamed MALIN. *1933:* Sold to A/B Deep Sea Trader (K. Hansen manager), Finland and renamed ESBO. *19.10.1935:* Stranded on Selter Rocks whilst on a voyage from Preston to Finland in ballast. *26.3.1936:* Refloated and taken in tow but sank later in the day when 4 miles S. of Ailsa Craig. She was bound for Troon where she was to have been broken up by the West of Scotland Shipbreaking Co. Ltd.

AVRISTAN *Author's Collection*

B.15 ARMANISTAN (I) (1901)
2298g, 1466n. 302.6 × 43.2 × 19.8 feet.
T3-cyl. by Central Marine Engine Works, West Hartlepool.
22.12.1900: Launched and *1.1901* completed by Wm. Gray and Co. Ltd., West Hartlepool (Yard No. 627) for Anglo-Algerian Steamship Co. (1896) Ltd. *1901:* Sold to Sifneo Fréres, Greece and renamed ZANOS SIFNEO, *1919:* Sold to Oriental Shipping Co. Ltd. (A. A. Capparis manager), Greece. *1926:* Sold to G. Z. Gounaris, Greece and renamed GIANNOULIS GOUNARIS. *2.5.1940:* Stranded off Foreland Point, North Devon whilst on a voyage from Cardiff to Marseilles. *8.7.1940:* Refloated and taken in tow bound for Briton Ferry to be broken up by T. W. Ward Ltd.

Contract price £35,250 including £7800 for machinery. Payable in cash on completion or $\frac{1}{3}$ in cash on delivery and the balance payable over 4 years in equal $\frac{1}{2}$ yearly instalments plus interest at 5% per annum in advance. Security to be held in debentures in the owning company. The vessel to be secured by a mortgage on the whole boat and the vessel to be transferred to the purchaser pro rata as payments are made.

B.16 TURKISTAN (III) (1905-1910)
ON. 118717. 4505g, 2899n. 373.1 × 50.2 × 27.4 feet.
T3-cyl. by Central Marine Engine Works, West Hartlepool.
21.2.1905: Launched and *3.1905* completed by Wm. Gray and Co. Ltd., West Hartlepool (Yard No. 698) for Anglo-Algerian Steamship Co. (1896) Ltd. *1910:* Sold to Hamburg-Amerikanische Packetfahrt A. G., Germany and renamed EKBATANA. *5.11.1914:* Scuttled by Turkish forces in the Shatt el Arab in an attempt to block the advance of the British Army into Mesopotamia. The wreck was later blown up and cleared by the British Military.

Contract price £52,000 including machinery. Payable in cash on completion or $\frac{1}{3}$ in cash on delivery and the balance payable over 5 years in equal $\frac{1}{2}$ yearly instalments plus interest at 5% per annum in advance. Security to be held in debentures in the owning company. The vessel to be secured by a mortgage on the whole boat and the vessel to be transferred to the purchaser pro rata as payments are made.

B.17 GORJISTAN (II) (1905-1910)
ON. 118718. 4508g, 2900n. 373.2 × 50.2 × 27.4 feet.
T3-cyl. by Central Marine Engine Works, West Hartlepool.
22.3.1905: Launched and *5.1905* completed by Wm. Gray and Co. Ltd., West Hartlepool (Yard No.699) for Anglo-Algerian Steamship Co. (1896) Ltd. *1910:* Sold to Hamburg-Amerikanische Packetfahrt A.G., Germany and renamed PERSEPOLIS. *1915:* Interned at Massowah. *15.12.1915:* Requisitioned by the Italian Government and renamed BELLUNO. *1920:* Sold to Soc. Anon. Cooperativa Garibaldi, Italy and renamed PIETRO GORI. *1926:* Renamed PATRIA. *1931:* Renamed ORDINE. *1932:* Sold to Italian shipbreakers for 140,000 lire and broken up at Savona.

Contract price £52,000 including machinery. Payable in cash on completion or $\frac{1}{3}$ in cash on delivery and the balance payable over 5 years in equal $\frac{1}{2}$ yearly instalments plus interest at 5% per annum in advance. Security to be held in debentures in the owning company. The vessel to be secured by a mortgage on the whole boat and the vessel to be transferred to the purchaser pro rata as payments are made.

B.18 ARABISTAN (II) (1905-1911)
See ARABISTAN (II) (No. C.7).

B.19 LURISTAN (I) (1905)
See LURISTAN (I) (No. C.9).

B.20 TABARISTAN (II) (1905-1906)
See TABARISTAN (II) (No. C.8).

B.21 AFGHANISTAN (II) (1905-1912)
ON. 122801. 4443g, 2849n. 380.3 × 49.7 × 26.9 feet.
T3-cyl. by the shipbuilder.
28.8.1905: Launched and *9.1905* completed by Scott's Shipbuilding and Engineering Co. Ltd., Greenock (Yard No. 394) for Anglo-Algerian Steamship Co. (1896) Ltd. 1912: Sold to American-Levant Line Ltd. (Stanley and John Thompson managers), London and renamed RIVER DELAWARE. *1915:* Sold to Nautilus Steam Shipping Co. Ltd. (F. and W. Ritson managers), Sunderland and renamed ELDER BRANCH. *1932:* Sold for £2000 to Smith and Company, Port Glasgow and broken up.

B.22 GULISTAN (1905-1913)
ON. 122802. 4445g, 2849n. 380.3 × 49.7 × 26.9 feet.
T3-cyl. by the shipbuilder.
11.9.1905: Launched and *10.1905* completed by Scott's Shipbuilding and Engineering Co. Ltd., Greenock (Yard No. 395) for Anglo-Algerian Steamship Co. (1896) Ltd. *1.1.1913:* Transferred to Strick Line Ltd. *1913:* Sold to Borderdale Shipping Co. Ltd. (J. Little and Co. (Glasgow) Ltd. managers), Glasgow and renamed BORDERDALE. *1915:* Sold to Donaldson Line Ltd. (Donaldson Bros. Ltd. managers), Glasgow and renamed TRITONIA. *27.2.1917:* Torpedoed and sunk by a German submarine 20 miles N.W. by W. of Inishtearaght Island whilst on a voyage from St. John, N.B. and Halifax to Glasgow with horses and general cargo.

GULISTAN in British India Line colours *A. Duncan*

B.23 KURDISTAN (1906-1910)
ON. 122810. 2813g, 1741n. 330.8 × 43.2 × 14.3 feet.
T3-cyl. by the shipbuilder.
25.4.1906: Launched and *6.1906* completed by Clyde Shipbuilding and Engineering Co. Ltd., Port Glasgow (Yard No.268) for Anglo-Algerian Steamship Co. (1896) Ltd. *20.10.1910:* Foundered in heavy weather 60 miles from the Scilly Isles whilst on a voyage from Manchester to Basrah via Marseilles with general cargo. Ten of the crew got away in a boat which was picked up 26 hours later by the British sailing ship VINCENT, 1904/94. In the meantime eight of the ten men had died of exposure or had been washed overboard.

B.24 LURISTAN (II) (1906-1912)
ON. 124353. 3286g, 2072n. 358.0 × 44.9 × 16.3 feet.
T3-cyl. by D. Rowan and Co., Glasgow.
7.1906: Completed by Wm. Hamilton and Co. Ltd., Port Glasgow (Yard No. 187) for Anglo-Algerian Steamship Co. (1896) Ltd. *1912:* Sold to Crossburn Steamship Co. Ltd. (Munson Steamship Line managers), Glasgow. *1914:* Renamed MUNDALE and transferred to Munson Steamship Line, U.S.A. *1916:* Transferred to Mundale Steamship Corporation, U.S.A. *1923:* Sold to Les Cargos Algeriens Soc. Anon., France and renamed MITIDJA. *8.11.1942:* Bombed and sunk during an air attack on Oran.

B.25 SHAHRISTAN (II) (1906-1911)
ON. 124354. 2811g, 1741n. 330.8 × 43.2 × 14.4 feet.
T3-cyl. by the shipbuilder.
4.7.1906: Launched and *8.1906* completed by Clyde Shipbuilding and Engineering Co. Ltd., Port Glasgow (Yard No. 269) for Anglo-Algerian Steamship Co. (1896) Ltd. *1911:* Sold to Moss Steam Ship Co. Ltd. (J. Moss and Co. managers), Liverpool and renamed SIPTAH. *1930:* Sold for £15,000 to A. Bernstein, Germany and renamed TRAUNSTEIN. *1937:* Transferred to Arnold Bernstein Schiffahrtsgesellschaft m.b.H. (Red Star Linie G.m.b.H. managers), Germany. *1938:* Transferred to Red Star Linie G.m.b.H., Germany. *1939:* Sold to Robert Bornhofen, Germany and renamed LUISE BORNHOFEN. 1939: Interned at Fayal, Azores. 1943 Sold to Companhia de Navegacao Carregadores Acoreanos, Portugal and renamed SETE CIDADES. *1950:* Sold to British Iron and Steel Corporation and allocated to Thos. Young and Sons (Shipbreakers) Ltd. who commenced demolition *14.8.1950* at Sunderland.

B.26 REGISTAN (I) (1906-1908)
ON. 124356. 2847g, 1775n. 331.8 × 43.2 × 14.4 feet.
T3-cyl. by the shipbuilder.
22.8.1906: Launched and *9.1906* completed by Gourlay Bros. and Co. (Dundee) Ltd., Dundee (Yard No. 222) for Anglo-Algerian Steamship Co. (1896) Ltd. *1908:* Sold to Compagnie Generale Transatlantique, France and renamed CARAIBE. *1935:* Sold to Wah Shang Steamship Co. Ltd. (Yih Zeu Fong manager), China and renamed HA-YIH. Subsequently captured by Japanese forces and operated for the Japanese Government by Daido Kaiun K.K. under the name KAIYOKU. *20.2.1939:* Struck rocks off the east coast of Santo Island, Korea whilst on a voyage from Karatsu to Tsingtao in ballast and subsequently sank.

B.27 TABARISTAN (III) (1906-1907)
ON. 124357. 3286g, 2072n. 358.0 × 44.9 × 16.3 feet.
T3-cyl. by D. Rowan and Co., Glasgow.
8.9.1906: Launched and *10.1906* completed by Wm. Hamilton and Co. Ltd., Port Glasgow (Yard No. 188) for Anglo-Algerian Steamship Co. (1896) Ltd. *1907:* Sold to Cia. Cubana de Nav. (New York & Cuba Mail Steamship Co. managers), Cuba and renamed SANTIAGO. *1914:* Transferred to New York & Cuba Mail Steamship Co., U.S.A. *11.3.1924:* Abandoned 60 miles south of Cape Hatteras whilst on a voyage from Cienfuegos to New York with a cargo of sugar.

TANGISTAN *G. Scott Collection*

B.28 TANGISTAN (I) (1906-1913)
ON. 124358. 3738g, 2393n. 350.0 × 42.2 × 16.3 feet.
T3-cyl. by Central Marine Engine Works, West Hartlepool.
19.9.1906: Launched and *10.1906* completed by Wm. Gray and Co. Ltd., West Hartlepool (Yard No. 736) for Anglo-Algerian Steamship Co. (1896) Ltd. *1.1.1913:* Transferred to Strick Line Ltd. *9.3.1915:* Torpedoed and sunk 9 miles north of Flamborough Head by the German submarine U.12 whilst on a voyage from Benisaf to Middlesbrough with a cargo of iron ore. There was only one survivor from the crew of 39 men.

Contract price £41,700 including machinery. Payable ½ (later reduced to ⅓) in cash on completion and the balance payable over 3 years in equal ½ yearly instalments. Security to be held in debentures in the owning company.

BARDISTAN in British India Line colours *R. Bigrigg Collection*

B.29 BARDISTAN (IV) (1906-1912)
ON. 124359. 3888g, 2501n. 360.1 × 50.2 × 16.8 feet.
T3-cyl. by the shipbuilder.
29.9.1906: Launched and *11.1906* completed by Scott's Shipbuilding and Engineering Co. Ltd., Greenock (Yard No. 407) for Anglo-Algerian Steamship Co. (1896) Ltd. *1912:* Sold to American-Levant Line Ltd. (Stanley and John Thompson managers), London and renamed RIVER MEANDER. *1.12.1912:* Foundered about 300 miles south of Halifax N.S. whilst on a voyage from New York to Mediterranean ports with general cargo.

TABARISTAN *Author's Collection*

B.30 TABARISTAN (IV) (1907-1913)
ON. 124714. 3883g, 1836n. 390.0 ×46.0 × 24.4 feet.
T3-cyl. by the shipbuilder.
15.6.1907: Launched and *7.1907* completed by D. and W. Henderson and Co. Ltd., Glasgow (Yard No. 461) for Anglo-Algerian Steamship Co. (1896) Ltd. *1.1.1913:* Transferred to Strick Line Ltd. *29.1.1913:* Sold to The Admiralty and converted to a destroyer depot ship. *10.1915:* Commissioned as H.M.S. DILIGENCE. *15.10.1926:* Sold to Hughes Bolckow Shipbreaking Co. Ltd. and *4.11.1926* arrived at Blyth to be broken up.

B.31 BALTISTAN (I) (1910-1912)
ON. 128911. 3297g, 2037n. 350.1 × 46.5 × 22.4 feet.
T3-cyl. by Central Marine Engine Works, West Hartlepool.
26.3.1910: Launched and *6.1910* completed by Wm. Gray and Co. Ltd., West Hartlepool (Yard No. 777) for Anglo-Algerian Steamship Co. (1896) Ltd. *1912:* Sold to Howard Smith Co. Ltd., Melbourne and renamed SAROS. *1913:* Transferred to Australian Steamships Ltd. (Howard Smith Co. Ltd. managers), Melbourne. *1914:* Transferred to Australian Steamships Proprietary Ltd. (same managers). *25.12.1937:* Wrecked off Cape Everard whilst on a voyage from Geelong to Sydney, N.S.W. with general cargo.

Contract price £37,800 including machinery. Payable $\frac{1}{3}$ on delivery and the balance of £25,200 payable over 5 years in equal $\frac{1}{2}$ yearly instalments plus interest at 5% per annum in advance. Security to be held in debentures in the owning company. The vessel to be secured by a mortgage on the whole boat and the vessel to be transferred to the purchaser pro rata as payments are made.

BALTISTAN as **SAROS** *W. Foote*

B.32 REGISTAN (II) (1910-1911)
ON. 128914. 3293g, 2034n. 350.7 × 46.5 × 22.4 feet.
T3-cyl. by Central Marine Engine Works, West Hartlepool.
9.5.1910: Launched and *7.1910* completed by Wm. Gray and Co. Ltd., West Hartlepool (Yard No. 778) for Anglo-Algerian Steamship Co. (1896) Ltd. *1911:* Sold to Cia. Cubana de Nav. (New York & Cuba Mail Steamship Co. managers), Cuba and renamed GUANTANAMO. *1914:* Transferred to New York & Cuba Mail Steamship Co., U.S.A. *1927:* Sold to New York & Porto Rico Steamship Co. Inc., U.S.A. and renamed COMERIO. *1934:* Sold to Agwilines Inc. (New York & Porto Rico Steamship Co. Inc. managers), U.S.A. *1940:* Sold to G. Bozzo fu L., Italy and renamed VITTORIN. *12.1941:* Seized at Norfolk, Va., operated by the United States Maritime Commission under the Panamanian flag and renamed GREY LAG. *1943:* Transferred to United States War Shipping Administration under the U.S. flag. *1946:* Sold to China Merchants Steam Navigation Co., China and renamed HAI LUNG. *1960:* Sold to Formosan shipbreakers who commenced demolition *19.1.1960.*

Contract price £37,800 including machinery. Payable ⅓ on delivery and the balance of £25,200 payable over 5 years in equal ½ yearly instalments plus interest at 5% per annum in advance. Security to be held in debentures in the owning company. The vessel to be secured by a mortgage on the whole boat and the vessel to be transferred to the purchaser pro rata as payments are made.

B.33 ARMANISTAN (III) (1911-1912)
ON. 128920. 3502g, 2163n. 360.0 × 47.1 × 22.8 feet.
T3-cyl. by Central Marine Engine Works, West Hartlepool.
2.1.1911: Launched and *2.1911* completed by Wm. Gray and Co. Ltd., West Hartlepool (Yard No. 786) for Anglo-Algerian Steamship Co. (1896) Ltd. *1912:* Sold to Hamburg — Amerikanische Packetfahrt Actien Gesellschaft, Germany and renamed DUALA. *2.8.1914:* Sailed from Las Palmas and *15.8.1914* joined the German auxiliary cruiser KAISER WILHELM DER GROSSE as a supply ship. *21.8.1914:* Returned to Las Palmas and interned. *9.6.1919:* Surrendered as a prize and allocated to the French Government. *1921:* Sold to Cie. Nantaise de Nav. a Vap., France and renamed MARTINIÈRE. *1939:* Sold to Cie. Generale Transatlantique, France and reduced to a storage hulk at Lorient. *6.1940:* Sank at Lorient following a fire and subsequently taken over by German forces and fitted out as a floating anti-aircraft battery. *8.1944:* Heavily damaged and sunk at Lorient. *1945:* Taken over by the French Navy for use as a hulk. *1955:* Sold to French shipbreakers and broken up at St. Nazaire.

Contract price £40,200 including machinery. Payable ⅓ on delivery and the balance of £26,800 payable over 3 years in equal ½ yearly instalments plus interest at 5% per annum in advance. Security to be held in debentures in the owning company.

AVRISTAN *A. Duncan*

B.34 AVRISTAN (II) (1911-1913)
ON. 112833. 3818g, 2447n. 360.0 × 46.0 × 17.9 feet.
T3-cyl. by J Dickinson and Sons Ltd., Sunderland.
22.3.1901: Launched and *4.1901* completed by Bartram and Sons, Sunderland (Yard No. 182) as IMOGEN for Howard Steam Ship Co. Ltd. (C. Howard and Sons managers), London. *1911:* Purchased by Anglo-Algerian Steamship Co. (1896) Ltd. and renamed AVRISTAN. *1.1.1913:* Transferred to Strick Line Ltd. *7.12.1916:* Torpedoed and sunk 14 miles S. by W. of Ushant by the German submarine U.21 whilst on a voyage from Portland (Me.) and Sydney (C.B.) to London with a cargo of wheat. One member of the crew was lost.

B.35 NIGARISTAN (II) (1911-1912)
ON. 128924. 4505g, 2864n. 373.0 × 50.0 × 27.5 feet.
T3-cyl. by Richardsons, Westgarth and Co. Ltd., West Hartlepool.
29.5.1911: Launched and *7.1911* completed by Irvine's Shipbuilding and Dry Docks Co. Ltd., West Hartlepool (Yard No. 505) for Anglo-Algerian Steamship Co. (1896) Ltd. *1912:* Sold to Hamburg-Amerikanische Packetfahrt Actien Gesellschaft, Germany and renamed MARKOMANNIA. *8.1914:* Taken over at Tsingtau and fitted out for service as a collier. *13.8.1914:* Joined the Cruiser Squadron under the command of Admiral Graf von Spee and attached to the cruiser EMDEN. *12.10.1914:* Captured and sunk by H.M.S. YARMOUTH off Simaur Island.

B.36 GORJISTAN (III) (1911-1913)
ON. 128925. 4537g, 2879n. 373.0 × 50.1 × 27.5 feet.
T3-cyl. by Central Marine Engine Works, West Hartlepool.
29.5.1911: Launched and *8.1911* completed by Wm. Gray and Co. Ltd., West Hartlepool (Yard No. 794) for Anglo-Algerian Steamship Co. (1896) Ltd. *1913:* Sold to Hamburg — Amerikanische Packetfahrt Actien Gesellschaft, Germany and renamed LIGURIA. *8.1914:* Interned at Pisagua, Chile. *8.8.1915:* Part of the cargo of copper, cocoa and hides discharged. *1.3.1916:* Vessel allowed into the bay for engine trials. *1917:* Engines destroyed by the crew. *9.1918:* Taken over by the Chilean military but unable to proceed to sea. *1920:* Returned in tow to Hamburg and repaired. *29.7.1921:* Surrendered to Great Britain as a prize. *1922:* Sold to Hamburg-Amerikanische Packetfahrt Actien Gesellschaft, Germany. *1933:* Sold for 13,809 marks to Deutsche Werft and broken up at Finkenwerder.

Contract price £52,800 including machinery. Payable in cash on completion or ⅓ in cash on delivery and the balance payable over 5 years in equal ½ yearly instalments or, at the purchaser's option, ½ in cash on delivery and the balance payable over 4 years in equal ½ yearly instalments. Interest payable at 5% per annum in advance and security to be held in debentures in the owning company.

B.37 TURKISTAN (IV) (1911-1913)
ON. 128929. 4523g, 2869n. 373.0 × 50.0 × 27.4 feet.
T3-cyl. by Central Marine Engine Works, West Hartlepool.
25.9.1911: Launched and *11.1911* completed by Wm. Gray and Co. Ltd., West Hartlepool (Yard No. 797) for Anglo-Algerian Steamship Co. (1896) Ltd. *1913:* Sold to Hamburg-Amerikanische Packetfahrt Actien Gesellschaft, Germany and renamed NINIVE. *8.1914:* Interned at Padang. *28.9.1919:* Surrendered to Great Britain as a prize and allocated to The Shipping Controller (British India Steam Navigation Co. Ltd. managers). *28.2.1921:* Purchased by Strick Line Ltd. and renamed SHAHRISTAN. *1922:* Transferred to Shahristan Steamship Co. Ltd. *1934:* Sold for £12,500 to Rederi A/B Atlanta (B. Krogius manager), Finland and renamed ATLANTA. *1938:* Sold to Finland-Amerika Linjen O/Y (same manager), Finland. *1939:* Renamed EQUATOR. *6.12.1941:* Stranded whilst on a voyage from Lulea to a German port. Subsequently refloated but sank near Sundsvall in a position 65.20N, 22.15E. *7.1942:* Salved, and after repairs, returned to service. *1952:* Sold to Finska Angfartygs A/B Finland and renamed ARATOR. 1953: Sold to A/B. Anchor Shipping Co. O/Y (C. H. Ericcson manager), Finland and renamed TRAMONTANA. *1956:* Sold to Santa Irini Cia. Maritima Ltda., Costa Rica and renamed IRINI. *1959:* Transferred to Panamanian flag. *6.2.1959:* Wrecked off Bats in the River Scheldt whilst on a voyage from Antwerp to Rijeka with a cargo of fertilizer and broke in two the following day.

Contract price £53,500 including machinery. Payable in cash on completion or ⅓ in cash on delivery and the balance payable over 5 years in equal ½ yearly instalments or, at the purchaser's option, ½ in cash on delivery and the balance payable over 4 years in equal ½ yearly instalments. Interest payable at 5% per annum in advance and security to be held in debentures in the owning company.

ARABISTAN in British India Line colours *F. Hawks*

B.38 ARABISTAN (III) (1912-1913)
ON. 128930. 5192g, 3307n. 400.0 × 53.5 × 27.1 feet.
T3-cyl. by Central Marine Engine Works, West Hartlepool.
19.3.1912: Launched and *5.1912* completed by Wm. Gray and Co. Ltd., West Hartlepool (Yard No. 802) for Anglo-Algerian Steamship Co. (1896) Ltd. *1.1.1913:* Transferred to Strick Line Ltd. *1913:* Sold to British India Steam Navigation Co. Ltd., Glasgow and renamed CHINDWARA. *1933:* Sold to shipbreakers for £7,250 and broken up in Japan.

Contract price £57,500 including £16,750 for machinery. Payable £27,500 in cash on completion and the balance of £30,000 payable over 5 years from the date of delivery in equal ½ yearly instalments plus interest at 5% per annum in advance. Security to be held in debentures in the owning company.

B.39 SHARISTAN (1912)

ON. 128934. 5254g, 3312n. 400.0 × 53.5 × 27.1 feet.
T3-cyl. by Central Marine Engine Works, West Hartlepool.
17.6.1912: Launched and *7.1912* completed by Wm. Gray and Co. Ltd., West Hartlepool (Yard No. 805) for Anglo-Algerian Steamship Co. (1896) Ltd. *1912:* Sold to Nederlandsche-Amerikaansche Stoomvaart Maats., Holland and renamed ZUIDERDIJK. *1918:* Taken over by the United States Shipping Board (Emergency Fleet Corporation), U.S.A. *1919:* Returned to owners. *1922:* Sold to The Law Shipping Co. Ltd. (T. Law and Co. managers), Glasgow and renamed MISTY LAW. *1932:* Sold for £11,250 to Achille Lauro, Italy and renamed EDERA. *1948:* Sold to Francesco Pittaluga fu Giacomo, Italy. *1956:* Sold to Cia. Mar. Caribe, Costa Rica and renamed FRIN. *1956:* Sold for £85,000 to Linea Adriatico Gulfo Persa Ltda., Costa Rica and renamed MAHFUZ. *1957:* Sold to "Sidemar" and *20.11.1957* arrived at Trieste to be broken up.

Contract price £57,500 including £16,750 for machinery. Payable £27,500 in cash on completion and the balance of £30,000 payable over five years from the date of delivery in equal ½ yearly instalments plus interest at 5% per annum in advance. Security to be held in debentures in the owning company. Payment for the engines was made in instalments as follows:

1st. instalment paid 1.3.11.	*Discount 2%*	*Cheque £3283*	*£3350*
2nd. instalment paid 3.7.12.	*Discount 2%*	*Cheque £3283*	*£3350*
3rd. instalment paid 3.7.12.	*Discount 2%*	*Cheque £3283*	*£3350*
4th. instalment paid 28.8.12.	*Discount 2%*	*Cheque £3283*	*£3350*
5th. instalment paid 28.8.12.	*Discount 2%*	*Cheque £3283*	*£3350*

SHARISTAN as **MISTY LAW** *A. Duncan*

B.40 CAMBYSES (1912-1913)
ON. 119873. 3184g, 2045n. 350.1 × 46.1 × 23.6 feet.
T3-cyl. by Central Marine Engine Works, West Hartlepool.
17.5.1905: Launched and *6.1905* completed by Wm. Gray and Co. Ltd., West Hartlepool (Yard No. 705) as CAMBYSES for Gladstone and Co., West Hartlepool. *1912:* Purchased by Anglo-Algerian Steamship Co. (1896) Ltd. *1.1.1913:* Transferred to Strick Line Ltd. and renamed ALBISTAN. *1919:* Sold to Pentaff Steam Ship Co. Ltd. (David P. Barnett and Co. managers), Cardiff. *1920:* Sold to Vernco Steam Ship Co. Ltd. (W. H. Vernall and Co. managers), London. *1921:* Sold to Rederi A/S Triton (T. Nielsen manager), Denmark. *1922:* Management transferred to O. Ovesen. *1924:* Sold to D/S A/S Patria (same manager), Denmark and renamed DUBLIN. *1925:* Sold Britain Steam Ship Co. Ltd. (Watts, Watts and Co. Ltd. managers), London for £13,500 and renamed FULHAM. *1934:* Sold to Delta Steam Ship Co. Ltd., London for £5000 and renamed FARNHAM. *1936:* Sold to Soc. Anon. Sbarchi, Imbarchi & Trasporti, Italy and renamed APOLLO. *1948:* Sold to Soc. Generale per l'Industria Mineraria & Chimica Montecatini, Italy. *1961:* Sold to Sidemar S.p.A. and *25.7.1961* arrived at Trieste to be broken up.

Contract price £33,250 including machinery. Payable $\frac{1}{2}$ in cash on completion and the balance payable over 4 years with bills being drawn each 6 months and renewed from time to time to fall in with this arrangement. Interest at 5% per annum payable in advance. The purchasers agree to hand the builders satisfactory security for the unpaid portion.

KOHISTAN in British India Line colours *W.S.P.L.*

B.41 KOHISTAN (I) (1912-1913)
ON. 127936. 4732g, 2949n. 395.5 × 51.5 × 17.9 feet.
T3-cyl. by G. Clark Ltd., Sunderland.
1.7.1908: Launched and *10.1908* completed by J. L. Thompson and Sons Ltd., Sunderland (Yard No. 466) as BEDOUIN for Bedouin Steam Navigation Co. Ltd. (W. and R. Thomson managers), Liverpool. *1912:* Purchased by Anglo-Algerian Steamship Co. (1896) Ltd., and renamed KOHISTAN *1.1.1913:* Transferred to Strick Line Ltd. *22.11.1917:* Torpedoed and sunk 25 miles W.$\frac{1}{2}$ S. of Marittimo Island by the German submarine UC35 whilst on a voyage from Rangoon to London with general cargo.

B.42 SEISTAN (I) (1912-1913)
ON. 123779. 4238g, 2712n. 364.0 × 50.0 × 17.9 feet.
T3-cyl. by Central Marine Engine Works, West Hartlepool.
17.12.1906: Launched and *2.1907* completed by Wm. Gray and Co. Ltd., West Hartlepool (Yard No. 737) as HEADLEY for Mitre Shipping Co. Ltd. (Houlder, Middleton and Co. managers), London. *1912:* Purchased by Anglo-Algerian Steamship Co. (1896) Ltd., and renamed SEISTAN. *1.1.1913:* Transferred to Strick Line Ltd. *23.10.1917:* Torpedoed and sunk 3½ miles N. by W. ¼ W. from Flamborough Head by the German submarine UB 57 whilst on a voyage from the River Tyne to Falmouth with a cargo of coal. Five of the crew were lost.

Contract price £45,600 including machinery. Payable ½ in cash on completion and the balance payable over 2 years in equal ½ yearly instalments plus interest at 5% per annum in advance. The builders to hold satisfactory security.

BAHARISTAN *A. Duncan*

B.43 BAHARISTAN (I) (1912-1913)
ON. 128935. 3629g, 2291n. 360.0 × 51.0 × 22.7 feet.
T3-cyl. by Central Marine Engine Works, West Hartlepool.
14.8.1912: Launched and *9.1912* completed by Wm. Gray and Co. Ltd., West Hartlepool (Yard No. 814) for Anglo-Algerian Steamship Co. (1896) Ltd. *1.1.1913:* Transferred to Strick Line Ltd. *1914:* Sold to Romania Primiere Soc. Nationale de Nav. Maritima, Roumania and renamed SIRETUL. *1935:* Sold to A. Vlasov, Roumania. *1941:* Transferred to the Panamanian flag and renamed OMEGA. *1942:* Taken over by the Ministry of War Transport (Navigation and Coal Trade Co. Ltd., managers), London. *1947:* Sold to Cia. Argentina de Nav. Ultramar S.A., Panama. *1948:* Sold to Soc. Italiana Trasport Marittimi, Italy and renamed CASTELBRUNO, *1952:* Renamed CASTEL BRUNO. *1953:* Sold to Italian shipbreakers and *13.3.1953* arrived at Trieste to be broken up.

Contract price £46,000 including £10,200 for machinery. Payable net cash on completion and on 13.6.1912 *the owners wrote to the builders referring to....a cheque for £25,000 posted to you on 11th. inst. on a/c of purchase price....you are to allow us interest of 4% per annum on this up to date of delivery.*

B.44 SHAHRISTAN (III) (1913)
ON. 133099. 4949g, 3105n. 405.0 × 52.5 × 27.5 feet.
T3-cyl. by Blair and Co. Ltd., Stockton on Tees.
23.12.1912: Launched by Richardson, Duck and Co. Ltd., Stockton on Tees (Yard No. 629) for Anglo-Algerian Steamship Co. (1896) Ltd. and *2.1913* completed as CHANTALA for British India Steam Navigation Co. Ltd., Glasgow. *5.4.1916:* Torpedoed and sunk 15 miles North of Cape Bengut by the German submarine U34 whilst on a voyage from Middlesbrough and London to Calcutta with general cargo.

ANGLO-ARABIAN AND PERSIAN STEAMSHIP CO. LTD.

This Company was formed in 1892 to build and operate vessels in the U.K.-Persian Gulf trade. Loading ports were South Wales ports, London, Manchester, Glasgow, Antwerp and Marseilles. Discharging ports included Port Sudan, Djibouti, Aden, Muscat, Bushire and Basrah, with other smaller Arabian and Persian ports as cargo offered. In 1905 this Company was merged with Anglo-Algerian Steamship Co. (1896) Ltd.

The livery, which was probably adopted with the building of the first ship for this company, was similar in all respects to that of the Anglo-Algerian Steamship Co. (1896) Ltd. and the vessels were given similar names.

C.1 ARABISTAN (I) (1893-1901)
ON. 98203. 3194g, 2045n. 325.0 × 42.0 × 18.9 feet.
T3-cyl. by the shipbuilder.
17.4.1893: Launched and *4.1893* completed by A. Stephen and Sons, Glasgow (Yard No. 343) for Anglo-Arabian and Persian Steamship Co. Ltd. *1901:* Sold to Bucknall Nephews, London. *1910:* Sold to F. Chiama & Danove, Italy and renamed GIANO. *24.12.1911:* Wrecked 15 miles from Tobruk, on the coast of Cyrenaica, whilst on a voyage from Augusta with a cargo of coal.

TURKISTAN *W.S.P.L.*

C.2 FARSISTAN (I)/TURKISTAN (I) (1894-1898)
ON. 98208. 4060g, 2612n. 345.0 × 47.0 × 26.7 feet.
T3-cyl. by the shipbuilder.
5.7.1894: Launched as FARSISTAN and *8.1894* completed as TURKISTAN by A. Stephen and Sons, Glasgow (Yard No. 352) for Anglo-Arabian and Persian Steamship Co. Ltd. *10.1.1898:* Sold to British and Colonial Steam Navigation Co. Ltd. (Bucknall Bros. managers), London and renamed BEIRA. *1900:* Transferred to Bucknall Steamship Lines Ltd. (same managers). *1910:* Sold to Kishimoto Kisen Kabushiki Kaisha, Japan and renamed SHINKAI MARU. *1915:* Sold to K. Shida (Mitsui Bussan Kaisha managers), Japan and renamed YUBARI MARU. *1921:* Sold to Hokkaido Tanko Kisen Kabushiki Kaisha, Japan. *1930:* Sold to Sugaya K.K., Japan and renamed MIHARU MARU. *1935:* Sold to shipbreakers.

C.3 TURKISTAN (II) (1898-1904)
ON. 109643. 3204g, 1992n. 350.0 × 45.0 × 16.2 feet.
T3-cyl. by Central Marine Engine Works, West Hartlepool.
1.9.1898: Launched and *12.1898* completed by Wm. Gray and Co. Ltd., West Hartlepool (Yard No. 566) for Anglo-Arabian and Persian Steamship Co. Ltd. *1904:* Sold to G. de Zaldo (New York & Cuba Mail Steamship Co. managers), Cuba and renamed BAYAMO *1906:* Sold to Cia. Cubana de Nav. (same manager), Cuba. *1914:* Transferred to New York & Cuba Mail Steamship Co., U.S.A. *1923:* Sold to shipbreakers.

Contract price £37,500 including £12,600 for machinery. Payable in cash on completion or $\frac{1}{2}$ on delivery and the balance payable over 3 years in equal $\frac{1}{2}$ yearly instalments plus interest of 5% per annum in advance. Security to be held in debentures in the owning company. The vessel to be secured by a mortgage on the whole boat.

C.4 GORJISTAN (I) (1900-1904)
ON.109649. 3261g, 2093n. 350.0 × 45.1 × 16.3 feet.
T3-cyl. by Central Marine Engine Works, West Hartlepool.
28.6.1900: Launched and *9.1900* completed by Wm. Gray and Co. Ltd., West Hartlepool (Yard No. 613) for Anglo-Arabian and Persian Steamship Co. Ltd. *1904:* Sold to H. R. Matthaei, Germany. *1904:* Sold to the Russian Navy and converted to a floating workshop by Blohm & Voss. *1905:* Delivered to the Russian Navy and renamed ANGARA. *1918:* Withdrawn from service. *1923:* Renamed SERP-I-MOLOT. *28.8.1941:* Bombed and heavily damaged by German aircraft during the evacuation of Tallinn (Reval). Beached near Suursaari in the Gulf of Finland and abandoned as a total loss.

Contract price £47,150 including £14,750 for machinery. Payable in cash on completion or $\frac{1}{2}$ in cash on delivery and the balance payable over 3 years in equal $\frac{1}{2}$ yearly instalments plus interest at 6% per annum in advance. Security to be held in debentures in the owning company. The vessel to be secured by a mortgage on the whole boat.

C.5 TABARISTAN (I) (1900-1902)
ON. 109650. 3430g, 2206. 368.0 × 45.1 × 16.3 feet.
T3-cyl. by Central Marine Engine Works, West Hartlepool.
11.10.1900: Launched and *11.1900* completed by Wm. Gray and Co. Ltd., West Hartlepool (Yard No. 620) for Anglo-Arabian and Persian Steamship Co. Ltd. *1902:* Sold to J. T. Rennie and Son, Aberdeen and renamed INKONKA. *1911:* Sold to Charente Steamship Co. Ltd. (T. and J. Harrison managers), Liverpool. *1919:* Sold to D. MacIver and Co. Ltd., Liverpool and renamed TUSCANY. *1929:* Sold to The West of Scotland Shipbreaking Co. Ltd. for £7700 and broken up at Troon.

Contract price £53,500 including £17,000 for machinery. Payable in cash on completion or $\frac{1}{3}$ in cash on delivery and the balance payable over 3 years in equal $\frac{1}{2}$ yearly instalments plus interest at 5% per annum in advance. Security to be held in debentures in the owning company. The vessel to be secured by a mortgage on the whole boat and the vessel to be transferred to the purchaser pro rata as payments are made.

C.6 ESTHER (1901-1906)
ON. 63696. 347g, 206n. 145.5 × 25.7 × 10.1 feet.
Two cyl. steam engine by the shipbuilder.
1864: Completed by Auguste Cochot, Paris as ESTHER for his own account. *1871:* Sold to Jules Gaudet, London. *1873:* Transferred to Gaudet Frères, London. *1887:* Sold to E. J. Hough, London. *1888:* Sold to J. T. Hutchins (J. T. Short manager), London. *1889:* Sold to C. H. Pile, London. *1889:* Sold to London and South Wales Steamship Co. Ltd., London. *1892:* Sold to Francis Moore, London. *1892:* Sold to M. E. Rodocanachi, London. *1892:* Sold to R. Clarence Gillchrest, London. *7.1901:* Purchased by Anglo-Arabian and Persian Steamship Co. Ltd. 1906: Sold to shipbreakers.

C.7 ARABISTAN (II) (1901-1905)
ON. 113765. 2891g, 1819n. 324.0 × 47.1 × 21.7 feet.
T3-cyl. by G. Clark Ltd., Sunderland.
26.10.1901: Launched and *11.1901* completed by Wm. Pickersgill and Sons, Sunderland (Yard No. 136) for Anglo-Arabian and Persian Steamship Co. Ltd. *20.7.1905:* Transferred to Anglo-Algerian Steamship Co. (1896) Ltd. *1911:* Sold to Bank of Athens (L. Nicolaides manager), Greece and renamed EUXEINOS. *1913:* Sold to L. Nicolaides, Greece. *2.3.1918:* Torpedoed and sunk by the German submarine UB53 near Kassandra in the Aegean Sea.

C.8 TABARISTAN (II) (1903-1905)
ON. 118713. 3398g, 2173n. 358.0 × 45.0 × 16.3 feet.
T3-cyl. by Central Marine Engine Works, West Hartlepool.
7.10.1903: Launched and *11.1903* completed by Wm. Gray and Co. Ltd., West Hartlepool (Yard No. 676) for Anglo-Arabian and Persian Steamship Co. Ltd. *20.7.1905:* Transferred to Anglo-Algerian Steamship Co. (1896) Ltd. *1906:* Sold to G. de Zaldo (J. E. Ward & Co. managers), Cuba. *1907:* Renamed CAMAGUEY. *1907:* Sold to Cia. Cubana de Nav. (New York & Cuba Mail Steamship Co. managers), Cuba. *1914:* Transferred to New York & Cuba Mail Steamship Co., U.S.A. *1934:* Sold to shipbreakers.

Contract price £40,500 including machinery. Payable in cash on completion or $\frac{1}{3}$ in cash on delivery and the balance payable over 4 years in equal $\frac{1}{2}$ yearly instalments plus interest at 5% per annum in advance.

C.9 LURISTAN (I) (1904-1905)
ON. 118714. 3398g, 2174n. 358.0 × 45.0 × 16.3 feet.
T3-cyl. by Central Marine Engine Works, West Hartlepool.
19.11.1903: Launched and *1.1904* completed by Wm. Gray and Co. Ltd., West Hartlepool (Yard No. 677) for Anglo-Arabian and Persian Steamship Co. Ltd. *20.7.1905:* Transferred to Anglo-Algerian Steamship Co. (1896) Ltd. *1905:* Sold to G. de Zaldo (J. E. Ward & Co. managers), Cuba. *1906:* Renamed ANTILLA. *1907:* Sold to Cia. Cubana de Nav. (New York & Cuba Mail Steamship Co. managers), Cuba. *1914:* Transferred to New York & Cuba Mail Steamship Co., U.S.A. *1930:* Reduced to a barge.

Contract price £40,500 including machinery. Payable in cash on completion or $\frac{1}{3}$ in cash on delivery and the balance payable over 4 years in equal $\frac{1}{2}$ yearly instalments plus interest at 5% per annum in advance.

LA COMMERCIALE STEAM NAVIGATION CO. LTD.

This Company was formed in 1905 and the vessels registered under it's ownership ran in conjunction with those of the Anglo-Algerian Steamship Co. (1896) Ltd. in the U.K. to Mediterranean and the U.K.-Gulf trades. On 1st January 1913 the company merged with the Anglo-Algerian Steamship Co. (1896) Ltd. to form Strick Line Ltd.
The livery was similar to that worn by the Anglo-Algerian Steamship Co. (1896) Ltd. fleet and the vessels had similar Gulf place names.

D.1 ARMANISTAN (II) (1905-1906)
ON. 118719. 4002g, 2605n. 360.0 × 50.2 × 17.0 feet.
T3-cyl. by the shipbuilder.
13.7.1905: Launched and *8.1905* completed by D. and W. Henderson and Co. Ltd., Glasgow (Yard No. 446) for La Commerciale Steam Navigation Co. Ltd. *22.1.1906:* Sold to Dampfschiffs-Reederei Union A. G., Germany and renamed WELLGUNDE. *23.11.1912:* Sold to Continentale Rhederei A. G., Germany and renamed HEIMFELD. *21.1.1914:* Sold to Deutsche Levante Linie, Germany and renamed PERA. *1919:* Surrendered to Great Britain as a prize and allocated to The Shipping Controller (Bell, Symondson and Co. managers), London. *1921:* Sold to Bolton Steam Shipping Co. Ltd. (F. Bolton and Co. managers), London and renamed RUBENS. *1927:* Sold to P. J. Corcodilos, Greece for £22,000 and renamed IOANNIS CORCODILOS. *1933:* Sold to Italian shipbreakers for £4100.

ARMANISTAN *W.S.P.L.*

D.2 BARDISTAN (III) (1905-1906)
ON. 122804. 4044g, 2603n. 360.1 × 50.3 × 17.0 feet.
T3-cyl. by D. Rowan and Co., Glasgow.
20.10.1905: Launched and *11.1905* completed by Wm. Hamilton and Co. Ltd., Port Glasgow (Yard No. 180) for La Commerciale Steam Navigation Co. Ltd. *12.5.1906:* Sold to Dampfschiffs-Reederei Union A. G., Germany and renamed WOGLINDE. *23.11.1912:* Sold to Continentale Rhederei A. G., Germany and renamed MANSFELD. *29.10.1913:* Sold to Deutsche Levante Linie, Germany and renamed GALATA. *1.8.1914:* Arrived at Lisbon and subsequently interned. *23.2.1916:* Requisitioned by the Portuguese Government and renamed FARO. *1924:* Sold to Cia. Colonial de Navegacao, Portugal and renamed BENGUELA. *1933:* Sold to Italian shipbreakers for £3500.

SERBISTAN *W.S.P.L.*

D.3 SERBISTAN (I) (1906-1913)
See SERBISTAN (I) (No. B.11).

D.4 NIGARISTAN (I) (1906-1907)
See NIGARISTAN (I) (No. B.7)

THE DWINA LTD.

This Company was formed in 1905 to acquire and operate ships on an unusual, almost unseen but very special service. Ships owned by the company were stationed at the entrance to the Shatt el Arab river and met incoming ships of the ocean going fleets. There, outside the bar, they took cargo from the ships, sufficient to lighten them to a draught of about 20 feet, to enable them to cross the bar and proceed up river. Both ships then proceeded to destination. Vessels bought for the company were all small and elderly but performed sterling service. By 1928 the bar had been dredged and a proper deep channel made and marked, and the lightening service was no longer needed, so the last vessel was sold, but that was far from being the end of the company. Barges, lighters and other small craft were needed to service ships in the river and the Dwina Ltd. operated these right up to the 1960's.

The livery was similar to that of the Anglo-Algerian Steamship Co. (1896) Ltd. but no special nomenclature was ever adopted and vessels kept the names they were bought with.

A steel 'Thames' type barge called DWINA II was the last craft owned by the company.

E.1 DWINA (1905-1909)
See DWINA (No. A.2).

E.2 RAITHWAITE HALL (1909-1929)
ON. 54573. 723g, 445n. 200.3 × 28.8 × 16.9 feet.
Two cylinder steam engine by an unknown builder. Replaced in 1874 by a C.2-cyl. by T. Richardson and Sons, Hartlepool.
6.1868: Launched by Denton, Gray and Co., West Hartlepool (Yard No. 75) as RAITHWAITE HALL for George Pyman and Co., West Hartlepool. *1878:* Sold to Pyman, Bell and Co., Newcastle. *1906:* Sold to T. Pallister and Co., Newcastle. *10.1906:* Sold to Wm. France, Fenwick and Co. Ltd., London. *5.5.1909:* Purchased by The Dwina Ltd. *1929:* Sold to shipbreakers.

RAITHWAITE HALL *B. Spaldin Collection*

E.3 NEGHILEH (1919-1921)
ON. 51065. 774g, 442n. 226.8 × 28.0 × 15.7 feet.
Two cylinder steam engine by the shipbuilder. Replaced in 1880 by a C.2-cyl. by Day, Summers and Co., Southampton.
10.1864: Launched by Barclay, Curle and Co., Glasgow (Yard No. 124) as MORAY for John Warrack and Co., Leith. *1865:* Sold to Khedivial Steamship Administration, Egypt and renamed NEGHILEH. *1899:* Transferred to Khedivial Mail Steamship & Graving Dock Co., London. *1919:* Purchased by The Dwina Ltd. *1921:* Sold to Cie. Maritime de l' Afrique Orientale, France. *1923:* Sold to shipbreakers.

E.4 TREGOTHNAN (1926-1928)
See TREGOTHNAN (No. K.5).

TREGOTHNAN *W.S.P.L.*

STRICK LINE LTD.

Formed on 1st January 1913 by a merger of Anglo-Algerian Steamship Co. (1896) Ltd. and La Commerciale Steam Navigation Co. Ltd. this company was to operate the U.K. and Continent to Persian Gulf trade.

Twelve vessels were transferred from the ownership of the two previous companies and from henceforth the Gulf trade was run as a completely separate operation from the Mediterranean trade, which, by this time, was operated by the La Tunisienne Steam Navigation Co. Ltd. formed in 1909.

The livery was the same as that worn by the previous companies in the Gulf trade and the names also carried on the tradition of the past twenty years.

In 1919 the Strick Line Ltd. with it's remaining ships was sold to P&O Steam Navigation Company but remained under the management of Frank C. Strick & Co. Ltd. In 1922 five vessels were transferred to three new companies and in the following year Strick Line (1923) Ltd. was formed.

F.1 MURISTAN (I) (1913)
See MURISTAN (I) (No. B.10).

F.2 SERBISTAN (I) (1913-1916)
See SERBISTAN (I) (No. B.11).

F.3 GULISTAN (1913)
See GULISTAN (No. B.22).

F.4 TANGISTAN (I) (1913-1915)
See TANGISTAN (I) (No. B.28).

F.5 TABARISTAN (IV) (1913)
See TABARISTAN (IV) (No. B.30).

TABARISTAN alongside Manchester Dry Docks Wharf *R. Fenton Collection*

F.6 AVRISTAN (II) (1913-1916)
See AVRISTAN (II) (No. B.34).

F.7 ARABISTAN (III) (1913)
See ARABISTAN (III) (No. B.38).

F.8 ALBISTAN (I) (1913-1919)
See CAMBYSES (No. B.40).

ALBISTAN as **FULHAM** *A. Duncan*

F.9 KOHISTAN (I) (1913-1917)
See KOHISTAN (I) (No. B.41).

F.10 SEISTAN (I) (1913-1917)
See SEISTAN (I) (No. B.42).

F.11 BAHARISTAN (I) (1913-1914)
See BAHARISTAN (I) (No. B.43).

F.12 BALUCHISTAN (II) (1913)
See BALUCHISTAN (II) (No. B.12).

F.13 ARABISTAN (IV) (1913)
ON. 128943. 5222g, 3295n. 400.2 × 53.6 × 27.2 feet.
T3-cyl. by Central Marine Engine Works, West Hartlepool.
4.7.1913: Launched and *8.1913* completed by Wm. Gray and Co. Ltd., West Hartlepool (Yard No. 827) for Strick Line Ltd. *1913:* Sold to British India Steam Navigation Co. Ltd., Glasgow and renamed CHINKOA. *1937:* Sold for £20,000 to Nailsea Steam Ship Co. Ltd. (E.R. Management Ltd. managers), Cardiff and renamed NAILSEA TOWER. *1937:* Sold for £12,000 to W. H. Arnott, Young and Co. Ltd., and broken up at Dalmuir.

Contract price £66,900 including machinery. Payable £5000 when keel laid, £6000 when framed, £6000 when plated, £3000 when launched, £6900 on completion and the balance of £40,000 payable over 4 years in equal ½ yearly instalments plus interest at 5% per annum in advance. The builders to allow interest at 4% per annum on instalments paid up to completion. Security to be held in debentures in the owning company.

NIGARISTAN as **PORTLOE** *G. Scott Collection*

F.14 NIGARISTAN (III) (1913-1918)
ON. 128940. 4345g, 2743n. 365.2 × 50.8 × 26.0 feet.
T3-cyl. by Central Marine Engine Works, West Hartlepool.
16.10.1913: Launched and *11.1913* completed by Wm. Gray and Co. Ltd., West Hartlepool (Yard No. 835) for Strick Line Ltd. *1918:* Sold to Portloe Steam Ship Co. Ltd. (W. E. Hinde and Co. managers), Cardiff. *1919:* Renamed PORTLOE. *1920:* Transferred to Portfield Steam Ship Co. Ltd. (same managers), Cardiff. *1932:* Sold for £9000 to Constants (South Wales) Ltd. (M. Constant manager), London. *1935:* Renamed LYMINGE. *1937:* Sold for £26,000 to Goulandris Brothers, Greece and renamed GEORGE J. GOULANDRIS. *29.6.1941:* Torpedoed and sunk west of the Canary Islands in a position 29.05 N, 25.10 W. by the German submarine U66 whilst on a voyage from Mauritius to Leith Roads with a cargo of sugar.

Contract price £52,800 including £11,500 for machinery. Payable £12,800 on completion and the balance of £40,000 payable over 5 years in equal ½ yearly instalments plus interest at 5% per annum in advance. Security to be held in debentures in the owning company.

F.15 SHAHRISTAN (VI) (1919-1920)
ON. 136153. 3127g, 1856n. 331.3 × 46.8 × 23.2 feet.
T3-cyl. by G. Clark Ltd., Sunderland.
27.4.1919: Launched by J. Priestman and Co., Sunderland (Yard No. 282) as WAR BEACON for The Shipping Controller and *7.1919* completed as SHAHRISTAN for Strick Line Ltd. *1920:* Sold to Union Steam Ship Company of New Zealand Ltd., Wellington and renamed KAWATIRI. *1936:* Sold for £9500 to S. Sakamoto, Japan but registered under Sun Wen Kwei (Kawasaki Kisen K. K. managers), China and renamed WEN YUAN. *1938:* Transferred to Sakamoto Shoji K. K., Japan and renamed SEIKAI MARU. *1940:* Sold to Kita Nippon K. K., Japan. *24.8.1942:* Torpedoed and sunk by the U.S. submarine GUARDFISH in a position 38.12 N, 141.30 E. whilst outward bound from Yokohama.

F.16 SERBISTAN (II) (1919-1922)
ON. 136154. 3072g, 1864n. 331.4 × 46.8 × 23.2 feet.
T3-cyl. by Richardsons, Westgarth and Co. Ltd., Middlesbrough.
15.7.1919: Launched by Sir Raylton Dixon and Co. Ltd., Middlesbrough (Yard No. 619) as WAR SURF for The Shipping Controller and *10.1919* completed as SERBISTAN for Strick Line Ltd. *1922:* Transferred to Serbistan Steamship Co. Ltd. *1926:* Sold for £25,750 to Kawasaki Kisen Kaisha, Japan and renamed URAJIO MARU. *1938:* Name rendered as URAZIO MARU. *30.12.1942:* Bombed and sunk by U.S. Army Air Corps aircraft off the Aleutian Islands in a position 51.58 N, 177.33 E.

F.17 WAR LARK/TURKISTAN (V) (1919-1922)
ON. 142635. 5194g, 3178n. 400.2 × 52.2 × 28.5 feet
T3-cyl. by the shipbuilder.
1918: Completed by Earle's Shipbuilding and Engineering Co. Ltd., Hull (Yard No. 632) as WAR LARK for The Shipping Controller (J. H. Welsford and Co. Ltd. managers), Liverpool. *10.1919:* Purchased by Strick Line Ltd. *1920:* Renamed TURKISTAN. *1922:* Transferred to Turkistan Steamship Co. Ltd. *1925:* Sold for £47,500 to D/S A/S Grey County (Willy Gilbert manager), Norway and renamed GREY COUNTY. *1929:* Sold for £37,000 to Lorentz W. Hansens Rederi A/S, Norway. *1937*: Sold to D/S A/S Songa (Klaus Wiese Hansen manager), Norway. *1947:* Sold to Rederi A/B Svenska Lloyd (K. R. Bokman manager), Sweden and renamed TITANIA. *1951:* Sold to Rederi A/B Transatlantic (Gunnar Carlsson manager), Sweden and renamed TOLKEN. *1951:* Sold for £214,300 to Rederi A/B Rex (Ragnar Kallstrom manager), Sweden and renamed RESARO. *1955:* Sold for £51,000 to Cia. de Nav. Miramar S.A., Liberia and renamed GEOWILKA. *1960:* Sold for £63,500 to Japanese shipbreakers and *17.9.1960* arrived at Osaka. Subsequently moved to Hirao where breaking was commenced *1.10.1960* by Matsukura Shoten K. K.

F.18 ARABISTAN (V) (1919-1922)
ON. 142446. 5205g, 3189n. 400.2 × 52.2 × 28.5 feet.
T3-cyl. by the shipbuilder.
1918: Completed by Earle's Shipbuilding and Engineering Co. Ltd., Hull (Yard No. 631) as WAR MAGPIE for The Shipping Controller (H. Samman and Co. managers), Hull. *11.1919:* Purchased by Strick Line Ltd. and renamed ARABISTAN. *1922:* Transferred to Serbistan Steamship Co. Ltd. *1926:* Sold for £42,500 to Kobe Sanbashi K. K., Japan and renamed KOHRYU MARU. *10.3.1928:* Wrecked during a typhoon 20 miles north of Inuboye whilst on a voyage from Everett, Washington to Yokohama with a cargo of timber. There were no survivors from her crew.

ARABISTAN *Author's Collection*

F.19 MURISTAN (III) (1920-1922)
ON. 136160. 3062g, 1877n. 331.3 × 46.8 × 23.2 feet.
T3-cyl. by G. Clark Ltd., Sunderland.
6.11.1919: Launched and *1.1920* completed by J. Priestman and Co., Sunderland (Yard No. 284) for Strick Line Ltd., having been laid down for The Shipping Controller. *1922:* Transferred to Turkistan Steamship Co. Ltd. *1926:* Sold for £25,750 to Kawasaki Kisen K. K., Japan and renamed TAKAO MARU. *9.5.1943:* Torpedoed and sunk by the U.S. submarine WAHOO in a position 38.57 N, 141.49 E. off Ofunato, Honshu Island, Japan.

F.20 SHAHRISTAN (VII) (1921-1922)
See TURKISTAN (IV) (No. B.37).

SHAHRISTAN *Author's Collection*

AVRISTAN *A. Duncan*

F.21 AVRISTAN (III) (1922-1923)
ON. 146669. 4453g, 2622n. 351.0 × 52.5 × 26.7 feet.
T3-cyl. by Central Marine Engine Works, West Hartlepool.
16.7.1920: Launched and *1.1921* completed by Wm. Gray and Co. (1918) Ltd., West Hartlepool (Yard No. 937) as SAINT RENE for Societe Navale de l'Ouest, France. 1922: Purchased by Strick Line Ltd. and renamed AVRISTAN. *1923*: Transferred to Strick Line (1923) Ltd. *1928*: Sold to Cie. Navale et Commerciale de l'Oceanie, France and renamed SAINT AUGUSTIN. *1930:* Sold to Societe des Services Contractuels des Messageries Maritimes, France and renamed ASTROLABE. *1935:* Sold to Cia. Genovese di Nav. a Vap. S.A., Italy and renamed CAPO LENA. *1942:* Taken over by the German Navy and renamed KAPOLENA. *18.8.1944:* Scuttled by German forces at St. Nazaire. *1951:* Wreck broken up.

F.22 REGISTAN (III) (1922-1923)
ON. 146678. 4449g, 2615n. 351.0 × 52.5 × 26.7 feet.
T3-cyl. by Central Marine Engine Works, West Hartlepool.
29.9.1920: Launched and *3.1921* completed by Wm. Gray and Co. (1918) Ltd., West Hartlepool (Yard No. 938) as SAINT ROGER for Societe Navale de l'Ouest, France. *1922:* Purchased by Strick Line Ltd. and renamed REGISTAN. *1923:* Transferred to Strick Line (1923) Ltd. *1928:* Sold to Cie. Navale et Commerciale de l'Oceanie, France and renamed SAINT ELOI. *1930:* Sold to Societe des Services Contractuels des Messageries Maritimes, France and renamed BOUSSOLE. *1935:* Sold to Compania Chilena de Navegacion Interoceanica, Chile and renamed ARAUCO. *17.4.1960:* Arrived at Yokohama and subsequently moved to Hirao to be broken up.

REGISTAN *A. Duncan*

SERBISTAN STEAMSHIP CO. LTD.

One of three companies founded by P&O Steam Navigation Company in 1922 to operate the Gulf trade of the Strick Line Ltd. which had been bought in 1919. Managed by Frank C. Strick & Co. Ltd. for P&O the vessels were indistinguishable from Strick Line ships in livery and name, but were in fact, wartime standard ships laid down for and purchased from the Shipping Controller. The ships were sold to Japanese companies in 1926 and the firm liquidated.

SERBISTAN *A. Duncan*

G.1 SERBISTAN (II) (1922-1926)
See SERBISTAN (II) (No. F.16)

G.2 ARABISTAN (V) (1922-1926)
See ARABISTAN (V) (No. F.18).

SHAHRISTAN STEAMSHIP CO. LTD.

One of three companies founded by P&O Steam Navigation Company in 1922 to operate the Gulf trade of the Strick Line Ltd. which had been bought in 1919. Managed by Frank C. Strick & Co. Ltd. for P&O the vessels had names and livery similar to those of the Strick Line.

In 1928 Mr. Strick, through London & Paris Steamship Co. Ltd., acquired 49% of the Shahristan Steamship Co. Ltd. and that part ownership continued until 1972, when P&O re-acquired the 49% minority holding and the company once more became a 100% subsidiary of P&O. On 19th April 1973 the last vessel in the fleet was transferred to the P&O General Cargo Division and the company went into liquidation.

After World War II, when company liveries were resumed, the hull colour did not return to the original black but remained grey, with the addition of a white apron. About 1960 the masts and derricks were changed from the original buff to grey, similar to the hull colour.

SHAHRISTAN *W.S.P.L.*

H.1 SHAHRISTAN (VII) (1922-1934)
See TURKISTAN (IV) (No. B.37).

NIGARISTAN *J. K. Byass*

H.2 NIGARISTAN (IV) (1922-1941)

ON. 139037. 5993g, 3752n. 421.7 × 56.2 × 29.7 feet.
T3-cyl. by the shipbuilder.
20.12.1912: Launched and *2.1913* completed by Bremer Vulkan Schiffbau und Maschinenfabrik, Vegesack (Yard No. 561) as RAPPENFELS for Deutsche Dampfschifffahrts Gesellschaft ''Hansa'', Germany. *8.8.1914:* Captured 8 miles south of Ceylon by H.M.S. ESPIEGLE and taken to Colombo. *1915:* Taken over by the Admiralty, renamed DIYATALAWA and placed under the management of Grahams and Co. *1920:* Transferred to The Shipping Controller (Director, India Office Shipping, manager). *1922:* Purchased by Shahristan Steamship Co. Ltd. for £52,250 and renamed NIGARISTAN. *24.9.1941:* Abandoned on fire in a position 57.55 N, 27.32 W. whilst on a voyage from Cochin to Liverpool.

H.3 GORJISTAN (IV) (1945-1960)

See GORJISTAN (IV) (No. K.11).

GORJISTAN as built *Author's Collection*

GORJISTAN in post war colours *A. Duncan*

H.4 KOHISTAN (III) (1945-1959)

See KOHISTAN (III) (No. K.12).

KOHISTAN *Author's Collection*

H.5 GOULISTAN (1960-1962)

See GOULISTAN (No. K.32).

GOULISTAN *G. Scott Collection*

MURISTAN with larger funnel *A. Duncan*

H.6 MURISTAN (IV) (1960-1966)
See MURISTAN (IV) (No. K.34).

H.7 NIGARISTAN (V) (1963-1967)
See NIGARISTAN (V) (No. K.27).

NIGARISTAN *W.S.P.L.*

H.8 SHAHRISTAN (X) (1965-1973)
ON. 306217. 9280g, 5212n, 12616d. 503′3″ × 67′8″ × 29′1″.
6-cyl. 2 S.C.S.A. oil engine by Wm. Doxford and Sons (Engineers) Ltd., Sunderland.
8.9.1964: Launched and *1.1965* completed by J. Readhead and Sons Ltd., South Shields (Yard No. 614) for Shahristan Steamship Co. Ltd. *5.1.1965:* Ran trials. *1.5.1972:* P&O General Cargo Division appointed managers. *19.4.1973:* Transferred to Peninsular and Oriental Steam Navigation Company. *31.1.1975:* Renamed STRATHAPPIN. *18.1.1979:* Sold to Rina Shipping Co. Ltd., Greece and renamed IRENES IDEAL. *1982:* Sold to Square Shipping Inc., Malta and renamed IDEAL. *19.9.1985:* Delivered to Burhani Metal Works Ltd., at Chittagong and *2.10.1985* demolition commenced at Bhatiyari Beach.

SHAHRISTAN *W.S.P.L.*

H.9 BALTISTAN (III) (1968-1972)
See BALTISTAN (III) (No. K.35).

BALTISTAN at Basrah *W.S.P.L.*

TURKISTAN STEAMSHIP CO. LTD.

One of three companies founded by P&O Steam Navigation in 1922 to operate the Gulf trade of the Strick Line Ltd., which had been bought in 1919. Managed by Frank C. Strick and Co. Ltd. for P&O the vessels of the company were indistinguishable from Strick Line ships in livery and name, but were, in fact, wartime standard ship laid down for the Shipping Controller. The last vessel was sold to Japan in 1926 and the company went in liquidation.

J.1 TURKISTAN (V) (1922-1925)
See TURKISTAN (V) (No. F.17).

TURKISTAN as **RESARO** *W.S.P.L.*

J.2 MURISTAN (III) (1922-1926)
See MURISTAN (III) (No. F.19).

STRICK LINE (1923) LTD.

STRICK LINE LTD.

This company was founded in 1923 by P&O Steam Navigation Company to replace the former Strick Line Ltd. and operate the Gulf trade. It carried on the traditions of previous Strick companies on the Gulf service and had similar names and liveries for it's ships.

In 1928 Mr. Strick, through the London & Paris Steamship Co. Ltd., purchased a 49% interest in Strick Line (1923) Ltd. and this part ownership continued until 1972, when the minority shareholding was purchased by P&O. Throughout it's history the company was managed by Frank C. Strick & Co. Ltd. and manned by Strick personnel.

In 1946 the company became Strick Line Ltd. and in October 1962 Strick Line Ltd. bought the management company Frank C. Strick & Co. Ltd. and it's subsidiaries. After World War II the hull colour was changed to grey with a white apron and about 1960, the masts and derricks were changed from the original buff to grey, similar to the hull colour.

Apart from the direct trade between U.K.-Continent and the Persian Gulf, ships of this company were regularly seen all over the world, especially after World War II. There had always been the regular carriage of dates during the season to New York, usually returning to the U.K. on a charter from U.S. East Coast Ports. There was also red oxide from Hormuz Island to several destinations, including Genoa and U.S. ports, and a large trade in Iraqi barley to many places, often for breweries. The main reason for ships being seen in India, Australia, Mauritius, South and East Africa, and other places however, was the nature of the Gulf trade. As the states around the Gulf developed their oil resources and their income increased, so their imports increased, but, apart from Iraq and Iran, there was no export trade except for the oil, so that only about one in four ships could find a homeward cargo after discharging. The only way the voyage homewards could be made to pay was via the charter market, either voyage or time charter, which involved loading in distant parts after a ballast passage and often even a second charter to eventually bring the vessel back to the U.K.

After the P&O takeover in March 1972, ships were gradually transferred to the General Cargo Division, the last ship being absorbed in February 1974, when the Strick Line Ltd. went out of existence.

K.1 AVRISTAN (III) (1923-1928)
See AVRISTAN (III) (No. F.21)

AVRISTAN *W.S.P.L*

K.2 REGISTAN (III) (1923-1928)
See REGISTAN (III) (No. F.22).

BARDISTAN *Author's Collection*

K.3 BARDISTAN (V) (1923-1928)
ON. 147461. 4357g, 2592n. 351.0 × 52.5 × 26.7 feet.
T3-cyl. by Central Marine Engine Works, West Hartlepool.
2.2.1923: Launched and *4.1923* completed by Wm. Gray and Co. Ltd., West Hartlepool (Yard No. 951) for Strick Line (1923) Ltd. *1928:* Sold to Cie. Navale et Commerciale de l' Océanie, France and renamed SAINT ROCH. *1930:* Sold to Société des Services Contractuels des Messageries Maritimes, France and renamed RECHERCHE. *1935:* Sold to Cia. Genovese di Nav. a Vap. S.A., Italy and renamed CAPO OLMO. *1940:* Seized by French authorities at Marseilles and handed over to Great Britain. Allocated to the Ministry of Shipping, later Ministry of War Transport (Moss Hutchison Line Ltd., Liverpool managers). *1944:* Management transferred to James Burness and Sons Ltd., London. *1945:* Handed over to the French Government (Worms et Cie. managers). *1946:* Renamed KOUFRA. *1948:* Sold to Les Cargos Algériens S.A., France and renamed MADALI. *1951:* Sold to Mazzella et Cie., France and renamed LEON MAZZELLA. *1954:* Sold for £63,000 to Rami Seferoglu, registered under Seferoglu ve Demirel Vapurculuk Sirketi, Turkey and renamed SEFEROGLU. *1976:* Broken up at Izmir by her owners who commenced demolition 20.11.1976.

The contract had been placed on 25.3.1918 by Société Navale de l' Ouest, France and subsequently cancelled. It was renegotiated with F. C. Strick and Co. Ltd. on 23.11.1922 at an agreed price of £56,000 of which £14,000 was payable in cash on signing the contract and the balance of £42,000 in cash on delivery.

K.4 KOHISTAN (II) (1923-1928)
ON. 147493. 4366g, 2598n. 351.0 × 52.5 × 26.7 feet.
T3-cyl. by Central Marine Engine Works, West Hartlepool.
4.4.1923: Launched and *6.1923* completed by Wm. Gray and Co. Ltd., West Hartlepool (Yard No.952) for Strick Line (1923) Ltd. *1928:* Sold to Cie. Navale et Commerciale de l' Océanie, France and renamed SAINT LUC. *1930:* Sold to Sociétè des Services Contractuels des Messageries Maritimes, France and renamed ESPERANCE. *9.1940:* Taken over at Aden by the Ministry of Shipping, later the Ministry of War Transport (British India Steam Navigation Co. Ltd., London, managers). *1945:* Returned to Compagnie des Messageries Maritimes, France. *1956:* Sold for £105,000 to Panamanian Oriental Steamship Corp. (Wheelock, Marden and Co. Ltd., managers), Panama and renamed BELLA. *1960:* Sold to Transportes Maritimos Mundiales S.A., Panama and renamed BANDUNG. *1963:* Sold to Fuji Marden and Co. Ltd., and broken up at Hong Kong. *1.2.1963:* Demolition commenced.

The contract had been placed on 25.3.1918 by Société Navale de l' Ouest, France and subsequently cancelled. It was renegotiated with F.C. Strick and Co. Ltd. on 23.11.1922 at an agreed price of £56,000 of which £14,000 was payable in cash on signing the contract and the balance of £42,000 in cash on delivery.

KOHISTAN *W.S.P.L.*

K.5 TREGOTHNAN (1923-1926)
ON. 115646. 3075g, 1983n. 323.0 × 47.1 × 23.7 feet.
T3-cyl. by the shipbuilder.
12.3.1903: Launched and *4.1903* completed by J. Readhead and Sons Ltd., South Shields (Yard No. 368) as TREGOTHNAN for The Hain Steamship Co. Ltd., St. Ives. *20.4.1903:* Ran trials. *1.8.1923:* Purchased by Strick Line (1923) Ltd. *1926:* Transferred to The Dwina Ltd. *1928:* Sold for £6000 to S.A.M. Killingbeck (M. Xydia manager), Egypt. *1932:* Sold to Samy Khouri (Costa Xydia & Son managers), Egypt. *1935:* Sold to Basile Sapovalos, Greece. *1939:* Sold to Palestine Transport and Shipping Co. Ltd. (N. W. Purvis manager), Palestine and renamed HAIFA TRADER. *1941:* Sold to Irish Shipping Ltd., Eire and renamed IRISH LARCH. *1949:* Sold for £25,000 to Mehmet Hilmi Daregenli Sirketi, Turkey and renamed SABAH. *1952:* Sold to Fuad Muradoglu ve Hilmi Daregenli Vapurculuk Sirketi, Turkey. *1958:* Sold to Sadikzade Nazim Ogullari Vapurculuk Komandit Sirketi, Turkey and renamed KERVAN. *27.7.1961:* Arrived at Trieste to be broken up by Fratelli Cosulich who commenced work in September 1961.

K.6 TABARISTAN (V) (1925-1941)
ON. 139041. 6251g, 3990n. 422.4 × 56.2 × 29.7 feet.
T3-cyl. by the shipbuilder.
13.12.1913: Launched and *1.1914* completed by Akt. Ges. ''Weser'', Bremen (Yard No. 202) as FRANKENFELS for Deutsche Dampfschifffahrts Gesellschaft ''Hansa'', Germany. *5.8.1914:* Detained at Calcutta. Taken over by the Admiralty and placed under the management of Grahams and Co. *1920:* Transferred to the Secretary of State for India in Council (Director, India Office Shipping, manager). *1925:* Purchased by Strick Line (1923) Ltd. for £40,000 and renamed TABARISTAN. *29.5.1941:* Torpedoed and sunk by the German submarine U38 in the North Atlantic in a position 06.31 N, 15.23 W whilst on a voyage from Busreh and Table Bay for Freetown and the U.K. with a cargo of pig iron and ground nuts.

TABARISTAN *Author's Collection*

K.7 ARABISTAN (VII)/BANDAR SHAHPOUR (1927-1943)
ON. 149811. 5236g, 3268n. 400.0 × 53.5 × 27.2 feet.
T3-cyl. by Central Marine Engine Works, West Hartlepool.
3.3.1927: Launched and *4.1927* completed by Wm. Gray and Co. Ltd., West Hartlepool (Yard No. 982) for Strick Line (1923) Ltd. *25.4.1927* Ran trials. *1929:* Renamed BANDAR SHAHPOUR at the request of the Shah of Persia when he performed the official opening ceremony at the new port of Bandar Shahpour. 30.4.1943: Torpedoed and sunk by the German submarine U 515 in a position 07.15 N, 13.49 W. between Takoradi and Freetown. She was on a voyage from Abadan, Mormugao and Takoradi for Freetown and the U.K. with 6768 tons of general cargo, including oil seeds, manganese ore, rubber and copra. One passenger was lost.

Contract price included £30,500 for machinery.

BANDAR SHAHPOUR *Author's Collection*

K.8 BAHARISTAN (II)/SELVISTAN (1928-1960)
ON. 160495. 5479g, 3482n. 415.0 × 54.2 × 27.6 feet.
T3-cyl. by the shipbuilder.
21.4.1928: Launched and *6.1928* completed by J. Readhead and Sons Ltd., South Shields (Yard No. 490) for Strick Line (1923) Ltd. *7.6.1928:* Ran trials. *1946:* Owners restyled as Strick Line Ltd. *1958:* Renamed SELVISTAN in order to release her original name to a vessel under construction. *1960:* Sold to Japanese shipbreakers for £62,000 and *16.7.1960* arrived at Osaka to be broken up by Miyachi Salvage Co. who began demolition at Sakai *23.7.1960.*

Contract price £97,279 including machinery.

BAHARISTAN *A. Duncan*

K.9 FLORISTAN (I) (1928-1942)
ON. 160549. 5478g, 3483n. 415.3 × 54.2 × 27.6 feet.
T3-cyl. by the shipbuilder.
19.6.1928: Launched and *8.1928* completed by J. Readhead and Sons Ltd., South Shields (Yard No. 491) for Strick Line (1923) Ltd. *11.8.1928:* Ran trials. *19.1.1942:* Wrecked 6 miles north of Oversay Light, west coast of Islay whilst on a voyage from Manchester to Freetown and Persian Gulf ports with general cargo and mails.

Contract price £97,289 including machinery.

FLORISTAN *South Tyneside Museum*

K.10 ARABISTAN (VIII) (1929-1942)
ON. 161272. 5874g, 3701n. 425.7 × 55.0 × 28.5 feet.
T3-cyl. with low pressure turbine by the shipbuilder.
6.6.1929: Launched and *8.1929* completed by J. Readhead and Sons Ltd., South Shields (Yard No. 496) for Strick Line (1923) Ltd. *27.7.1929:* Ran trials. *11.8.1942:* Captured by the German auxiliary cruiser MICHEL and sunk in a position 11.30 S, 26.00 W. Of the crew of 57 plus 10 gunners only the chief engineer and a cadet survived, having been held as prisoners of war in Japan until the end of the war. She was on a voyage from Busreh and Table Bay for Trinidad and New York with 3267 tons of general cargo including tobacco, fur skins, liquorice and steel.

Contract price £107,075 including machinery.

ARABISTAN *Author's Collection*

K.11 GORJISTAN (IV) (1929-1945)
ON. 161320. 5888g, 3710n. 425.6 × 55.0 × 28.5 feet.
T3-cyl. with low pressure turbine by the shipbuilder.
19.9.1929: Launched and *11.1929* completed by J. Readhead and Sons Ltd., South Shields (Yard No. 498) for Strick Line (1923) Ltd. *5.11.1929:* Ran trials. *1945:* Transferred to Shahristan Steamship Co. Ltd. *1960:* Sold to Japanese shipbreakers for £65,000 and *1.9.1960* arrived at Tokyo to be broken up by Nichimen Jitsugyo Co.
Contract price £107,730 including machinery.

GORJISTAN *South Tyneside Museum*

KOHISTAN *South Tyneside Museum*

K.12 KOHISTAN (III) (1930-1945)
ON. 161353. 5884g, 3708n. 425.8 × 55.0 × 28.5 feet.
T3-cyl. with low pressure turbine by the shipbuilder.
30.11.1929: Launched and *1.1930* completed by J. Readhead and Sons Ltd., South Shields (Yard No. 499) for Strick Line (1923) Ltd. *18.1.1930:* Ran trials. *1945:* Transferred to Shahristan Steamship Co. Ltd. *1959:* Sold to Japanese shipbreakers for £60,000 and 13.11.1959 arrived at Kure to be broken up by Yoshiura Zosen on behalf of Banno Tsusho K. K.

Contract price £108,180 including machinery.

REGISTAN *Author's Collection*

K.13 REGISTAN (IV) (1930-1942)
ON. 161381. 5886g, 3711n. 426.0 × 55.0 ×28.5 feet.
T3-cyl. with low pressure turbine by the shipbuilder.
30.1.1930: Launched and *3.1930* completed by J. Readhead and Sons Ltd., South Shields (Yard No. 500) for Strick Line (1923) Ltd. *14.3.1930:* Ran trials. *9.1940:* Requisitioned by the Admiralty for service as an ocean boarding vessel and fitted with two 6" guns. *11.1941:* Returned to owners. *28.9.1942:* Torpedoed and sunk about 200 miles E.N.E. of Tobago by the German submarine U332 whilst on a voyage from Basrah to Philadelphia with 1319 tons of general cargo. Eleven crew members and five gunners were lost.

Contract price £104,270 including machinery.

ARMANISTAN *Author's Collection*

K.14 ARMANISTAN (IV) (1937-1940)
ON. 165387. 6805g, 4194n. 453.9 × 58.5 × 29.6 feet.
T3-cyl. with low pressure turbine by the shipbuilder.
29.10.1936: Launched and *1.1937* completed by J. Readhead and Sons Ltd., South Shields (Yard No. 507) for Strick Line (1923) Ltd. *20.1.1937:* Ran trials. *3.2.1940:* Torpedoed and sunk off the coast of Portugal in a position 38.15N, 11.15W. by the German submarine U25. She was on a voyage from Antwerp to Busreh with 8300 tons of general cargo including sugar and iron rails. Her crew was rescued.

Contract price £120,257 including machinery.

K.15 BALTISTAN (II) (1937-1941)
ON. 165458, 6803g, 4194n. 453.9 × 58.5 ×29.6 feet.
T3-cyl. with low pressure turbine by the shipbuilder.
24.2.1937: Launched and *5.1937* completed by J. Readhead and Sons Ltd., South Shields (Yard No. 508) for Strick Line (1923) Ltd. *17.5.1937:* Ran trials. *27.2.1941:* Torpedoed and sunk by the Italian submarine MICHELE BIANCHI in a position 51.52N, 19.55W. She was on a voyage from Ellesmere Port for Table Bay with 6200 tons of military stores. Two crew were killed and 45 plus 4 passengers reported missing.

Contract price £121,599 including machinery.

BALTISTAN *Author's Collection*

K.16 SHAHRISTAN (VIII) (1938-1941)
ON. 166563. 6935g, 4228n. 454.0 × 58.5 × 29.5 feet.
T3-cyl. with low pressure turbine by the shipbuilder.
29.6.1938: Launched and *9.1938* completed by J. Readhead and Sons Ltd., South Shields (Yard No. 513) for Strick Line (1923) Ltd. *8.9.1938:* Ran trials. *29.7.1941:* Torpedoed by the German submarine U371 in a position 35.19N, 23.53W. and sank the next day. She was on a voyage from London and the River Clyde for Busreh with general cargo and Government stores. Thirty nine crew and 26 passengers were lost.

Contract price £160,101 including machinery.

SHAHRISTAN after launching *South Tyneside Museum*

SHAHRISTAN *Author's Collection*

TURKISTAN after launching *South Tyneside Museum*

TURKISTAN *Author's Collection*

TURKISTAN in post war colours *John Clarkson, Longton*

K.17 TURKISTAN (VI) (1939-1962)
ON. 167156, 6935g, 4228n. 454.0 × 58.5 × 29.5 feet.
T3-cyl. with low pressure turbine by the shipbuilder.
24.10.1938: Launched and *1.1939* completed by J. Readhead and Sons Ltd., South Shields (Yard No. 514) for Strick Line (1923) Ltd. *28.12.1938:* Ran trials. *1946:* Owners restyled as Strick Line Ltd. *1962:* Sold for £90,000 to Phoebus Kyprianou, Greece and renamed DEMOS. *22.7.1962:* Wrecked during a typhoon on Kasho To, near Formosa in a position 22.40N, 121.25E. whilst on a voyage from Pyongyang to Bangkok in ballast.

Contract price £160,193 including machinery.

AFGHANISTAN *W.S.P.L.*

K.18 AFGHANISTAN (III) (1940-1962)
ON. 167404. 6992g, 4245n. 454.0 × 58.5 × 29.5 feet.
T3-cyl. with low pressure turbine by the shipbuilder.
11.12.1939: Launched and *3.1940* completed by J. Readhead and Sons Ltd., South Shields (Yard No. 516) for Strick Line (1923) Ltd. *4.3.1940:* Ran trials. *1946:* Owners restyled as Strick Line Ltd. *1962:* Sold to Marprisa Cia. Nav. S.A., Greece and renamed SAMAREITIS. *1965:* Sold to Cia. Minotauros S.A., Liberia and renamed CYRENIAN. *1967:* Sold to Nan Feng Steel Enterprise Co. Ltd. and *14.3.1967* arrived at Kaohsiung to be broken up.

Contract price £180,572 including machinery plus £2,000 for war fittings.

K.19 BALUCHISTAN (III) (1940-1942)
ON. 167540. 6992g, 4245n. 454.0 × 58.5 × 29.5 feet.
T3-cyl. with low pressure turbine by the shipbuilder.
21.3.1940: Launched and *6.1940* completed by J. Readhead and Sons Ltd., South Shields (Yard No. 517) for Strick Line (1923) Ltd. *8.3.1942:* Torpedoed and then sunk by gunfire by the German submarine U68 in a position 04.13N, 08.32W. in the Gulf of Guinea. She was on a voyage from Basrah to U.K. via Table Bay and Freetown with a cargo of 8000 tons of dates.

Contract price £182,310 including machinery plus £2,000 for war fittings.

AVRISTAN *W.S.P.L.*

K.20 AVRISTAN (IV) (1942-1963)
ON. 168304. 7266g, 5060n. 428.8 × 56.5 × 35.5 feet.
3-cyl. 2S.C.S.A. oil engine by the shipbuilder.
29.4.1942: Launched and *7.1942* completed by Wm. Doxford and Sons Ltd., Sunderland (Yard No. 690) for Strick Line (1923) Ltd. *1946:* Owners restyled as Strick Line Ltd. *1963:* Sold to Monique Navigation Corp., Liberia and renamed PAULIA. *1966:* Sold to Victoria Ocean Transport Ltd., Liberia and renamed VICTORIA LOYAL. *1967:* Renamed GRAND LOYAL. *13.2.1970:* Arrived at Kaohsiung to be broken up by Hwa Zohg Steel & Iron Works Ltd.

BARDISTAN *W.S.P.L.*

K.21 BARDISTAN (VI) (1942-1963)
ON. 168365. 7264g, 5055n. 428.5 × 56.5 × 35.5 feet.
3-cyl. 2 S.C.S.A. oil engine by the shipbuilder.
25.9.1942: Launched and *12.1942* completed by Wm. Doxford and Sons Ltd., Sunderland (Yard No. 697) for Strick Line (1923) Ltd. *1946:* Owners restyled as Strick Line Ltd. *1963:* Sold to Mariner Ocean Transport Co. S.A., Liberia and renamed PACIFIC MARINER. *1966:* Renamed EASTERN ENTERPRISE. *20.5.1972:* Arrived at Kaohsiung to be broken up by Dong Yung Steel Enterprise Co. who began work *2.6.1972.*

ARABISTAN *John Clarkson, Longton*

K.22 ARABISTAN (IX) (1944-1963)
ON. 169861. 7369g, 5039n. 431.0 × 56.5 × 35.5 feet.
3-cyl. 2 S.C.S.A. oil engine by the shipbuilder.
24.1.1944: Launched and *5.1944* completed by Wm. Doxford and Sons Ltd., Sunderland (Yard No. 714) for Strick Line (1923) Ltd. *1946:* Owners restyled as Strick Line Ltd. *1963:* Sold to Cia. Pacifica Financiera S.A., Liberia and renamed PANAGIOTIS LEMOS. *1967:* Sold to Astromando Cia. Nav. S.A., Liberia and renamed POLYXENI. *1968:* Transferred to the Somali flag. *30.9.1968:* Beached in a position 25.12S, 46.48E. after striking an unidentified underwater object the previous day whilst on a voyage from Sundsvall to Bombay. Abandoned as a total loss.

FLORISTAN *W.S.P.L.*

K.23 FLORISTAN (II) (1944-1963)
ON. 169964. 7368g, 5033n. 431.0 × 56.5 × 35.5 feet.
3-cyl. 2 S.C.S.A. oil engine by the shipbuilder.
12.6.1944: Launched and *10.1944* completed by Wm. Doxford and Sons Ltd., Sunderland (Yard No. 718) for Strick Line (1923) Ltd. *1946:* Owners restyled as Strick Line Ltd. *1963:* Sold to Cia. de Nav. Bayano S.A., Panama and renamed UJE. *22.9.1973:* Gutted by fire which broke out in her engineroom whilst she was lying at Antwerp. Sold to Spanish shipbreakers and *23.10.1973* arrived in tow at Bilbao to be broken up by Remasa.

REGISTAN as **TRESILLIAN** *Author's Collection*

K.24 REGISTAN (V) (1944-1945)
ON. 180022. 7368g, 5039n. 431.0 × 56.5 × 35.5 feet.
3-cyl. 2 S.C.S.A. oil engine by the shipbuilder.
9.8.1944: Launched and *12.1944* completed by Wm. Doxford and Sons Ltd., Sunderland (Yard No. 720) for Strick Line (1923) Ltd. *1945:* Sold to The Hain Steamship Co. Ltd., London. *1946:* Renamed TRESILLIAN. *1950:* Sold to Peninsular and Oriental Steam Navigation Company (The Hain Steamship Co. Ltd. managers), London. *30.11.1954:* Capsized and sank when her cargo shifted in heavy weather 25 miles off Ballycotton, in a position 51.14N, 07.30W whilst on a voyage from Montreal to Avonmouth with a cargo of grain. Thirteen crew were rescued by the British tanker LIPARUS, 6473/48 but one man died from swallowing oil. A further four men were picked up by the British motorship ARDGLEN, 1044/53, making a total of sixteen survivors from a crew of forty.

SHAHRISTAN on trials *South Tyneside Museum*

SHAHRISTAN, with the barge **DWINA II** on deck *Skyfotos*

K.25 SHAHRISTAN (IX) (1945-1962)
ON. 180552. 7309g, 5139n. 431.2 × 56.3 ×35.6 feet.
T3-cyl. by the shipbuilder.
27.2.1945: Launched and *4.1945* completed by J. Readhead and Sons Ltd., South Shields (Yard No. 544) for Strick Line (1923) Ltd. *30.4.1945:* Ran trials. *1946:* Owners restyled as Strick Line Ltd. *1962:* Sold to Italian shipbreakers and *19.12.1962* arrived at Monfalcone to be broken up.

Contract price £236,601 including machinery.

K.26 SERBISTAN (III) (1947-1962)
ON. 180544. 7239g, 5197n. 423.1 × 57.1 × 34.8 feet.
T3-cyl. by Ellicott Machinery Corporation, Baltimore, Md.
22.4.1944: Launched by Bethlehem Fairfield Shipyard Inc., Baltimore, Md. (Yard No. 2359) as SAMGLORY for the United States War Shipping Administration and bareboat chartered to the Ministry of War Transport (Dodd, Thomson and Co. Ltd. managers). *1947:* Purchased by Strick Line Ltd. for £135,000 and renamed SERBISTAN. *1962:* Sold for £90,000 to Cia de Nav. Surava S.A. (Sebastiano Tuillier manager), Liberia and renamed CALYPSO. *1968:* Sold to Panamic Shipping Co. S.A., Liberia. *30.3.1969:* Arrived at Hong Kong to be broken up by Leung Yau Shipbreaking Co. Ltd.

SERBISTAN *John Clarkson, Longton*

K.27 NIGARISTAN (V) (1947-1963)

ON, 181557. 7173g, 4347n, 9733d. 458.2 × 58.8 × 29.5 feet.
T3-cyl. with low pressure turbine by the shipbuilder.
11.9.1946: Launched and *3.1947* completed by J. Readhead and Sons Ltd., South Shields (Yard No. 551) for Strick Line Ltd. *1963:* Transferred to Shahristan Steamship Co. Ltd. *1967:* Sold to Astro Ascendente Cia. Nav. S.A., Greece and renamed ASTROMAR. *1969:* Renamed ARIS. *7.10.1971:* Delivered to Chinese shipbreakers at Shanghai.

Contract price £345,000 including machinery.

TABARISTAN *W.S.P.L.*

K.28 TABARISTAN (VI) (1947-1968)
ON. 181634. 7173g, 4346n, 9,850d. 458.2 × 58.8 × 29.5 feet.
T3-cyl. with low pressure turbine by the shipbuilder.
21.11.1946: Launched and *6.1947* completed by J. Readhead and Sons Ltd., South Shields (Yard No. 553) for Strick Line Ltd. *30.5.1947:* Ran trials. *1968:* Sold to Asimi Maritime Co. Ltd., Greece and renamed ST. GRIGOROUSA. *1968:* Sold to Southern Shipping and Enterprises Co. Ltd., Hong Kong and renamed HAI NING. *16.11.1971:* Delivered at Canton to Chinese shipbreakers.

Contract price £349,267 including machinery.

REGISTAN *W.S.P.L.*

K.29 REGISTAN (VI) (1947-1964)
ON. 181789. 7173g, 4346n, 9,850d. 458.2 × 58.8 × 29.5 feet.
T3-cyl. with low pressure turbine by the shipbuilder.
1.9.1947: Launched and *12.1947* completed by J. Readhead and Sons Ltd., South Shields (Yard No. 555) for Strick Line Ltd. *3.12.1947:* Ran trials. *1964:* Sold for £87,000 to Lynnbrook Ltd., Bermuda and renamed AQUATIC. *1968:* Sold to Natal Shipping Co. S.A., Greece and renamed HERACLES. *1.7.1970:* Beached at Hong Kong with a fire in her cargo of coal. Subsequently refloated but found to be damaged beyond economical repair. *25.8.1970:* Delivered at Whampoa to Chinese shipbreakers.

Contract price £364,627 including machinery.

ALBISTAN *A. Duncan*

K.30 ALBISTAN (II) (1948-1971)
ON. 181919. 5516g, 3262n 8950d. 429.5 × 57.0 × 25.7 feet.
T3-cyl. by G. Clark (1938) Ltd., Sunderland.
12.12.1947: Launched and *6.1948* completed by Short Bros. Ltd., Sunderland (Yard No. 498) for Strick Line Ltd. The contract had been placed by Australasian United Steam Navigation Co. Ltd., Melbourne and taken over by Strick Line Ltd. prior to the laying of the keel. *2.7.1971:* Arrived at Hong Kong to be broken up by Lee Sing Co.

ARMANISTAN on trials *South Tyneside Museum*

ARMANISTAN with larger funnel *A. Duncan*

K.31 ARMANISTAN (V) (1949-1965)
ON. 183004. 8409g, 5072n, 10880d. 492.4 × 62.2 × 30.9 feet.
T3-cyl. with low pressure turbine by the shipbuilder.
30.11.1948: Launched and *4.1949* completed by J. Readhead and Sons Ltd., South Shields (Yard No. 561) for Strick Line Ltd. *21.4.1949:* Ran trials. *1965:* Sold to Conway Transport Corporation, Liberia and renamed CONWAY. *1967:* Sold to Manfiba Shipping Co. S.A., Greece and renamed MITERA MARIA. *1971:* Sold to Fouad A. Khayat & Co. (Internacional de Comercio y Navegacion S.A. managers), Somali Republic and renamed MARBELLA. *13.2.1973:* Damaged by fire which broke out in her engine room while she was lying at Karachi during a voyage from Port Sudan to Yokohama. *12.1973:* Sold to Dada Steel Mills and *6.1.1974* left Karachi for Gadani Beach to be broken up.

GOULISTAN with larger funnel *W.S.P.L.*

K.32 GOULISTAN (1950-1960)
ON. 183215. 8430g, 5058n. 492.4 × 62.2 × 30.9 feet.
T3-cyl. with low pressure turbine by the shipbuilder.
22.9.1949: Launched and *4.1950* completed by J. Readhead and Sons Ltd., South Shields (Yard No. 563) for Strick Line Ltd. *4.4.1950:* Ran trials. *1960:* Transferred to Shahristan Steamship Co. Ltd. *1962:* Sold to Eisen und Metall A.G. after suffering machinery damage and *8.10.1962* arrived at Bremerhaven to be broken up.

TANGISTAN *W.S.P.L.*

TANGISTAN with larger funnel *Skyfotos*

K.33 TANGISTAN (II) (1950-1972)
ON. 183273. 7383g, 4389n, 9745d. 458.2 × 58.8 × 29.5 feet.
T3-cyl. with low pressure turbine by the shipbuilder.
20.12.1949: Launched and *6.1950* completed by J. Readhead and Sons Ltd., South Shields (Yard No. 567) for Strick Line Ltd. *23.6.1950:* Ran trials. *13.3.1972:* Arrived at Kaohsiung to be broken up by Tung Seng Steel Co.

K.34 MURISTAN (IV) (1950-1960)
ON. 184271. 8408g, 5006n, 10760d. 492.4 × 62.2 × 30.9 feet.
T3-cyl. with low pressure turbine by the shipbuilder.
16.5.1950: Launched and *10.1950* completed by J. Readhead and Sons Ltd., South Shields (Yard No. 566) for Strick Line Ltd. *29.9.1950:* Ran trials. *1960:* Transferred to Shahristan Steamship Co. Ltd. *1966:* Sold to Achille P. Halcoussis, Greece and renamed LEONIS. *1968:* Sold to Korea Atlas Line, South Korea and renamed ATLAS TRADER. *1970:* Sold to Hualing Shipping Corporation, Liberia and renamed YALING. *1972:* Sold to Chen Tung Shipping Co. Ltd., Liberia. *17.5.1972:* Arrived at Kaohsiung to be broken up by Chi Shun Hwa Steel Co.

MURISTAN *Skyfotos*

K.35 BALTISTAN (III) (1953-1968)
ON. 185936. 7489g, 4388n, 9620d. 459.8 × 58.5 × 28.3 feet.
4-cyl. 2 S.C.S.A. oil engine by North Eastern Marine Engineering Co. (1938) Ltd., Newcastle.
14.4.1953: Launched and *7.1953* completed by J. Readhead and Sons Ltd., South Shields (Yard No. 573) for Strick Line Ltd. *23.7.1953:* Ran trials. *1968:* Transferred to Shahristan Steamship Co. Ltd. *1.5.1972:* P&O General Cargo Division appointed managers. *16.12.1972:* Sold to Thenamaris Corporation S.A. (Thenamaris Maritime Inc. managers), Cyprus and renamed ELINDIA. *1973:* Transferred to Panamanian registry and renamed GULF DIAMOND. *20.5.1974:* Stranded in the Gulf of Oman in a position 25.25 N, 59.10 E. whilst on a voyage from Karachi to Persian Gulf ports. *24.6.1974:* Refloated and sold to Pakistani shipbreakers. *1.9.1974:* Arrived at Gadani Beach to be broken up by Abbas Steel Industries.

BALTISTAN *W.S.P.L.*

KHUZISTAN *Skyfotos*

K.36 KHUZISTAN (1955-1973)
ON. 186174. 7523g, 4231n, 9600d. 477′11″ × 58′6″ × 26′1¾″.
4-cyl. 2 S.C.S.A. oil engine by North Eastern Marine Engineering Co. (1938) Ltd., Newcastle.
15.9.1954: Launched and *1.1955* completed by J. Readhead and Sons Ltd., South Shields (Yard No. 580) for Strick Line Ltd. *12.1.1955:* Ran trials *1.5.1972:* P&O General Cargo Division appointed managers. *31.1.1973:* Sold to Nilmore Ltd. (Anglo Eastern Shipping Co. Ltd., managers), Hong Kong and renamed FOOCHOW under the Somali flag. *1976:* Sold to Foochow Shipping Inc., Somali Republic. *30.5.1976:* Sustained serious engine damage whilst on a voyage from Penang to Tsingtao and *2.6.1976* arrived in tow at Singapore. *1977:* Sold to Chinese shipbreakers and *17.2.1977* left Singapore in tow bound for Whampoa to be broken up.

BALUCHISTAN *W.S.P.L.*

K.37 BALUCHISTAN (IV) (1956-1973)
ON. 187401. 8370g, 4827n, 10100d. 510′4″ × 62′6″ × 26′7″.
6-cyl. 2 S.C.S.A. Doxford oil engine by Wallsend Slipway Co. Ltd., Wallsend.
15.12.1955: Launched and *5.1956* completed by J. Readhead and Sons Ltd., South Shields (Yard No. 585) for Strick Line Ltd. *29.5.1956:* Ran trials. *1.5.1972:* P&O General Cargo Division appointed managers. *19.4.1973:* Transferred to Peninsular and Oriental Steam Navigation Company. *18.4.1975:* Renamed STRATHAIRLIE. *26.8.1977:* Arrived at Kaohsiung to be broken up and handed over to Tien Cheng Steel Co. on the following day.

SEISTAN on trials *South Tyneside Museum*

K.38 SEISTAN (II) (1957-1958)
ON. 187620. 7440g, 4334n, 9600d. 477'11" × 58'6" × 25'8".
4-cyl. 2 S.C.S.A. Doxford oil engine by Hawthorn, Leslie (Engineers) Ltd., Newcastle.
15.5.1957: Launched and *7.1957* completed by J. Readhead and Sons Ltd., South Shields (Yard No. 592) for Strick Line Ltd. 27.7.1957: Ran trials. *17.2.1958:* Fire broke out in No. 5 hold beneath the explosives magazine whilst on a voyage from London to Khorramshahr with general cargo which included 170 tons of explosives, fuses and detonators. *18.2.1958:* Anchored about 2 miles east of South Sitra Beacon, Bahrein where about 75 tons of explosives were discharged into a barge whilst attempts to extinguish the fire continued. *19.2.1958:* Fire spread to the magazine and the subsequent explosion destroyed the after part of the vessel and much of the superstructure. As a result of the explosion 53 members of the crew, including the master, and four men in a tug alongside lost their lives and the forepart finally sank. *5.2.1959:* After being raised the forepart left Bahrein in tow of the Dutch tug RODE ZEE 500/49 bound for Italy. *22.6.1959*: Arrived at Palermo en route to Catania where the forepart was broken up.

KARAGHISTAN on trials *Author's Collection*

K.39 KARAGHISTAN (1957-1973)
ON. 187678. 7150g, 4229n, 9466d. 477'11" × 58'6" × 25'8".
4-cyl. 2 S.C.S.A. Doxford oil engine by Hawthorn, Leslie (Engineers) Ltd., Newcastle.
30.7.1957: Launched and *11.1957* completed by J. Readhead and Sons Ltd., South Shields (Yard No. 593) for Strick Line Ltd. *12.11.1957:* Ran trials. *1.5.1972:* P&O General Cargo Division appointed managers. *9.2.1973:* Sold to Contoyannis Shipping Ltd., Cyprus and renamed CONSTANTINOS. *1974:* Transferred to Congroup Maritime Co. Ltd. (Contoyannis Shipping Ltd. managers), Cyprus. *1977:* Sold to Stolos Cia. S.A. (Tristar Marine Management S.A. managers), Greece and renamed ADMIRAL C. *13.9.1978:* Wrecked one mile off Pylos in a position 36.53 N, 21.40 E. after her steering gear had failed in heavy weather. On *15.9.1978* her back broke and *3.12.1978* she sank. She was on a voyage from Antwerp to Jeddah with general cargo.

FARSISTAN on trials *South Tyneside Museum*

K.40 FARSISTAN (II) (1959-1973)
ON. 300874. 9633g, 5271n, 13416d. 500'6" × 63'3" × 30'8¼".
6-cyl. 2 S.C.S.A. Doxford oil engine by Hawthorn, Leslie (Engineers) Ltd., Newcastle.
8.1.1959: Launched and *5.1959* completed by J. Readhead and Sons Ltd., South Shields (Yard No. 599) for Strick Line Ltd. *7.5.1959:* Ran trials. *1.5.1972:* P&O General Cargo Division appointed managers. *19.4.1973:* Transferred to Peninsular and Oriental Steam Navigation Company. *27.1.1975:* Renamed STRATHADDIE. *21.1.1978:* Sold to Cori Shipping Corporation, Liberia and renamed SOPHOCLES. *1981:* Sold to Maldives Shipping Ltd., Maldive Islands and renamed MALDIVE PRIDE. *1983:* Sold to Ushodaya Shipbreakers, India and *9.10.1983* arrived at Visakhapatnam to be broken up.

K.41 BAHARISTAN (III) (1959-11973)
ON. 300950. 8517g, 4750n. 10950d. 511′3″ × 63′6″ × 28′1$\frac{3}{4}$″.
6-cyl. 2 S.C.S.A. Doxford oil engine by Hawthorn, Leslie (Engineers) Ltd., Newcastle. *24.2.1959:* Launched and *7.1959* completed by Caledon Shipbuilding and Engineering Co. Ltd., Dundee (Yard No. 516) for Strick Line Ltd. *1.5.1972:* P&O General Cargo Division appointed managers. *19.4.1973:* Transferred to Peninsular and Oriental Steam Navigation Company. *4.4.1975:* Renamed STRATHAROS. *29.12.1977:* Sold to Chi Kong Nav. Inc., Panama and renamed CHI KONG. *30.7.1979:* Arrived at Kaohsiung to be broken up by Taiwan Ship Scrap Co. Ltd., who commenced work *25.8.1979*.

BAHARISTAN *W.S.P.L.*

KOHISTAN *Author's Collection*

K.42 KOHISTAN (IV) (1960-1973)
ON. 302528. 9423g, 5246n. 13446d. 500′6″ × 63′3″ × 30′8$\frac{1}{4}$″.
6-cyl. 2 S.C.S.A. Doxford oil engine by Hawthorn, Leslie (Engineers) Ltd., Newcastle. *11.7.1960:* Launched and *11.1960* completed by J. Readhead and Sons Ltd., South Shields (Yard No. 605) for Strick Line Ltd. *8.11.1960:* Ran trials. *1.5.1972:* P&O General Cargo Division appointed managers. *19.4.1973:* Transferred to Peninsular and Oriental Steam Navigation Company. *21.2.1975:* Renamed STRATHASLAK. *6.6.1978:* Sold to Hibiscus Shipping Corp., Greece and renamed QUINCY. *1983:* Sold to Five Star Shipping Co. Ltd., Pakistan and *19.1.1983* arrived at Gadani Beach to be broken up.

K.43 GORJISTAN (V) (1961-1973)
ON. 302779. 9449g, 5297n. 13147d. 500′6″ × 63′3″ × 30′8″.
6-cyl. 2 S.C.S.A. oil engine by Wm. Doxford and Sons (Engineers) Ltd., Sunderland. *1.5.1961:* Launched and *11.1961* completed by J. Readhead and Sons Ltd., South Shields (Yard No. 608) for Strick Line Ltd. *2.11.1961:* Ran trials. *1.5.1972:* P&O General Cargo Division appointed managers. *19.4.1973:* Transferred to Peninsular and Oriental Steam Navigation Company. *25.2.1975:* Renamed STRATHATLOW. *22.11.1978:* Sold to Egyptian International Shipping Corporation, Egypt and renamed NILE U. *1982:* Renamed NILE. *1983:* Sold to Haryana Steel Company, India, and *23.6.1983* arrived at Bombay to be broken up.

GORJISTAN *W.S.P.L.*

TURKISTAN *W.S.P.L.*

K.44 TURKISTAN (VII) (1963-1973)
ON. 304416. 9270g, 5188n. 12550d. 503′3″ × 65′9″ × 29′1″.
6-cyl. 2 S.C.S.A. oil engine by Wm. Doxford and Sons (Engineers) Ltd., Sunderland. *12.9.1962:* Launched and *1.1963* completed by J. Readhead and Sons Ltd., South Shields (Yard No. 611) for Strick Line Ltd. *15.1.1963:* Ran trials. *1.5.1972:* P&O General Cargo Division appointed managers. *19.4.1973:* Transferred to Peninsular and Oriental Steam Navigation Company. *21.2.1975:* Renamed STRATHASSYNT. *16.2.1978:* Sold to Amber Star Maritime S.A., Panama and renamed AMBER STAR. *1980:* Sold to Vietnam Ocean Shipping Co., Vietnam and renamed LUC NGAN. *24.6.1985:* Arrived at Aioi to be broken up by Ishikawajima Kogyo K.K.

FLORISTAN *G. Scott Collection*

K.45 FLORISTAN (III) (1965-1973)
ON. 306330. 9296g, 5118n, 12616d. 503′3″ × 67′8″ × 29′1″.
6-cyl. 2 S.C.S.A. oil engine by Wm. Doxford and Sons (Engineers) Ltd., Sunderland.
19.1.1965: Launched and *6.1965* completed by J. Readhead and Sons Ltd., South Shields (Yard No. 615) for Strick Line Ltd. *3.6.1965:* Ran trials. *1.5.1972:* P&O. General Cargo Division appointed managers. *19.4.1973:* Transferred to Peninsular and Oriental Steam Navigation Company. *25.2.1975:* Renamed STRATHALVIE. *30.11.1978:* Sold to Vanguard Bay Shipping Co. Ltd., Greece and renamed ALEXANDRA. *4.11.1982:* Suffered major damage when fire broke out in the engine room whilst lying at Luanda following a voyage from Havana and declared a constructive total loss. *1983:* Sold to Tien Cheng Steel Manufacturing Co. Ltd., Taiwan and *6.6.1983* left Luanda in tow. *20.9.1983:* Arrived at Kaohsiung to be broken up.

SERBISTAN *W.S.P.L.*

K.46 SERBISTAN (IV) (1966-1973)
ON. 308027. 8985g, 4894n, 11319d. 503'4" × 63'10" × 27'6".
6-cyl. 2 S.C.S.A. oil engine by Wm. Doxford and Sons (Engineers) Ltd., Sunderland. *9.11.1965:* Launched and *3.1966* completed by J. Readhead and Sons Ltd., South Shields (Yard No. 617) for Strick Line Ltd. *3.3.1966:* Ran trials. *1.5.1972:* P&O General Cargo Division appointed managers. *19.4.1973:* Transferred to Peninsular and Oriental Steam Navigation Company. *6.1.1975:* Renamed STRATHANGUS. *6.9.1978:* Sold to Hong Kong Islands Shipping Co. Ltd., Panama and renamed KELLET ISLAND. *1983:* Sold to Golden Line (Pte.) Ltd., Panama and renamed GOLDEN BEAR. *1988:* Sold to Taiwan shipbreakers and arrived *19.3.1988* at Kaohsiung.

REGISTAN *A. Duncan*

K.47 REGISTAN (VII) (1966-1973)
ON. 308226. 8819g, 4870n, 11380d. 503'5" × 63'10" × 27'6".
6-cyl. 2 S.C.S.A. oil engine by Doxford and Sunderland Shipbuilding and Engineering Co. Ltd., Sunderland.
24.3.1966: Launched and *8.1966* completed by J. Readhead and Sons Ltd., South Shields (Yard No. 618) for Strick Line Ltd. *3.8.1966:* Ran trials. *1.5.1972:* P&O General Cargo Division appointed managers. *19.4.1973:* Transferred to Peninsular and Oriental Steam Navigation Company. *7.3.1975:* Renamed STRATHANNA. *23.9.1978:* Sold to Hong Kong Ocean Shipping Co. Ltd., Panama and renamed TSING YI ISLAND. *1987:* Sold to Chi Hsiang Steel Enterprise Co. Ltd., Taiwan and *29.6.1987* arrived at Kaohsiung to be broken up.

K.48 ARMANISTAN (VI) (1968-1973)
ON. 304192. 8531g, 4542n, 11360d. 485′6″ × 63′2″ × 28′5½″.
6-cyl. 2 S.C.S.A. oil engine by Fairfield-Rowan Ltd, Glasgow.
3.11.1964: Launched and *3.1965* completed by Hawthorn Leslie (Shipbuilders) Ltd., Newcastle (Yard No. 745) as ELYSIA for Athel Line Ltd. (Anchor Line Ltd. managers), Glasgow. *1968:* Transferred to Anchor Line Ltd. *1968:* Purchased by Strick Line Ltd. and renamed ARMANISTAN. *1.5.1972:* P&O General Cargo Division appointed managers. *19.4.1973:* Transferred to Peninsular and Oriental Steam Navigation Company. *20.6.1975:* Renamed STRATHAVOCH. *20.9.1978:* Sold to Hong Kong Ocean Shipping Co. Ltd., Panama and renamed SHARP ISLAND. *1983:* Sold to China Dismantled Vessel Trading Corporation and *18.11.1983* arrived at Kaohsiung to be broken up. Demolition commenced *3.12.1983* by Chien Yu Steel Industrial Co. Ltd.

ARMANISTAN *W.S.P.L.*

K.49 TABARISTAN (VII) (1969-1974)
ON. 337161. 9627g, 5475n, 14385d. 510′10″ (inc. bulbous bow) × 69′10″ × 30′2″.
6-cyl. 2 S.C.S.A. oil engine by Doxford and Sunderland Shipbuilding and Engineering Co. Ltd., Sunderland.
17.1.1969: Launched and *5.1969* completed by Swan Hunter Shipbuilders Ltd., South Shields (Yard No. 9) for Strick Line Ltd. *1.5.1972:* P&O General Cargo Division appointed managers. *1974:* Transferred to Peninsular and Oriental Steam Navigation Company. *22.4.1975:* Renamed STRATHARLICK. *30.11.1978:* Sold to Corthian Shipping Corporation, Greece and renamed AEOLIAN STAR. *1981:* Sold to Asterix Maritime Co. S.A., Greece and renamed ANDROMEDA. *1986:* Sold to Leyte Shipping Co. Ltd., Malta. *1986:* Sold to Indian shipbreakers and *6.10.1986* arrived at Alang to be broken up.

TABARISTAN *Strick Line*

K.50 NIGARISTAN (VI) (1970-1974)

ON. 341050. 9778g, 5526n, 13416d. 510′10″ (inc. bulbous bow) × 69′10″ × 30′2¼″. 6-cyl. 2 S.C.S.A. oil engine by Doxford and Sunderland Shipbuilding and Engineering Co. Ltd., Sunderland.

4.6.1970: Launched and *11.1970* completed by Swan Hunter Shipbuilders Ltd., South Shields (Yard No. 32) for Strick Line Ltd. *1.5.1972:* P&O General Cargo Division appointed managers. *14.2.1974:* Transferred to Peninsular and Oriental Steam Navigation Company. *25.1.1975:* Renamed STRATHAIRD. *16.7.1979:* Sold to Amaril Shipping Corporation, Greece and renamed GARIFALIA C. *1983:* Sold to Seric Bay Shipping Co. Ltd., Greece and renamed GARIFALIA. *1984:* Renamed ARCTUS. *1986:* Sold to Chinese shipbreakers and *26.1.1986* left Gabes, Tunisia bound for Zhanjiang.

NIGARISTAN *W.S.P.L.*

LONDON & PARIS STEAMSHIP CO. LTD.

This company was founded in 1889 by Mr. F. C. Strick in association with M. Jules Mesnier, initially to finance the building of the ALPHONSE PARRAN.

It remained a finance company until 1898 when it became a shipowning company in it's own right, with the building of the PARIS. Seven ships were owned over the following eighteen years, and they were employed carrying bunker coal from South Wales to Le Havre, to fuel the liners of Cie. Generale Transatlantique.

The last vessel owned by the company was wrecked in November 1916, but the London & Paris Steamship and Investment Co. Ltd. as it later became known, remains in existence to the present day.

L.1 PARIS (I) (1898)
ON. 104957. 1052g, 574n. 230.0 × 32.2 × 14.2 feet.
T3-cyl. by North Eastern Marine Engineering Co. Ltd., Newcastle.
23.12.1897: Launched and *2.1898* completed by Wood, Skinner and Co, Newcastle (Yard No.68) for London & Paris Steamship Co. Ltd. *19.2.1898:* Ran trials. *26.5. 1898:* Sold to Red Cross Iquitos Steamship Co. Ltd., (R. Singlehurst and Co. managers), Liverpool and renamed UCAYALI. *1901:* Booth Steam Ship Co. Ltd., appointed managers. *1905:* Transferred to Iquitos Steam Ship Co. Ltd., (same managers), Liverpool. *1913:* Transferred to Booth Steam Ship Co. Ltd., Liverpool. *1914:* Sold to Leopold Walford and Co., London. *7.1915:* Renamed STANISLAS. *9.1915:* Transferred to Leopold Walford (London) Ltd., London. *16.2.1916:* Sold to George Gibson and Co. Ltd., Leith. *1933:* Sold to G. Riccardi, Italy and renamed PESCARA. *1937:* Sold to Societa Anonima Navigazione e Trasporti, Italy. *1953:* Transferred to Soc. per Azione Navigazione e Trasporti, Italy. *1960:* Sold to Italian shipbreakers.

PARIS *W.S.P.L.*

L.2 PARIS (II) (1900-1901)
ON. 109648. 1080g, 532n. 230.0 × 32.2 × 17.4 feet.
T3-cyl. by North Eastern Marine Engineering Co. Ltd., Newcastle.
12.5.1900: Launched and *6.1900* completed by Wood, Skinner and Co. Ltd., Newcastle (Yard No. 90) for London & Paris Steamship Co. Ltd. *9.6.1900:* Ran trials. *1901:* Sold to the French Navy for service as a naval auxiliary and renamed LOIRET. *1937:* Withdrawn and reported broken up.

PARIS *W.S.P.L.*

L.3 PARIS (III) (1902-1912)
ON. 113767. 1229g, 633n. 250.0 × 32.2 × 17.5 feet.
T3-cyl. by North Eastern Marine Engineering Co. Ltd., Newcastle.
7.4.1902: Launched and *5.1902* completed by Wood, Skinner and Co. Ltd., Newcastle (Yard No. 105) for London & Paris Steamship Co. Ltd. *1912:* Sold to N. V. Maatschappij tot Explotatie van het S. S. Willy (N. De Voogd, Jr, manager), Holland and renamed WILLY. *1914:* Management transferred to W. H. Berghuys Coal Trade. *1933:* Sold to Cia. Atlantica de Navagacao Ltda., Portugal and renamed BEIRIZ. *1936:* Sold to Andrade & Co. and broken up at Lisbon.

L.4 HAVRE (I) (1905-1912)
ON. 118720. 2024g, 1177n. 288.0 × 39.0 × 22.4 feet.
T3-cyl. by Central Marine Engine Works, West Hartlepool.
3.8.1905: Launched and *9.1905* completed by Wm. Gray and Co. Ltd., West Hartlepool (Yard No. 713) for London & Paris Steamship Co. Ltd. *1912:* Sold to Anglo-Saxon Petroleum Co. Ltd., London. *10.6.1942:* Torpedoed and sunk in the Mediterranean Sea between Alexandria and Mersa Matruh by the German submarine U431. She was on a voyage from Alexandria to Tobruk with 2125 tons of cased benzine. Eighteen crew and 2 gunners were lost.

Contract price £24,600 including machinery. Payable in cash on completion or $\frac{1}{3}$ on delivery and the balance over 3 years in equal $\frac{1}{2}$ yearly instalments plus interest at 5% per annum in advance. Security to be held in debentures in the owning company.

HAVRE *A. Duncan*

KARA *W.S.P.L.*

L.5 KARA (I) (1912-1916)
ON. 96669. 2338g, 1507n. 290.1 × 39.9 × 19.8 feet.
T3-cyl. by Blair and Co. Ltd., Stockton on Tees.
7.10.1889: Launched and *12.1889* completed by C. S. Swan and Hunter, Newcastle (Yard No. 144) as KARA for Mercantile Steam Ship Co. Ltd., London. *1912:* Purchased by London & Paris Steamship Co. Ltd. *10.7.1916:* Mined near Pakefield Gat Buoy whilst on a voyage from Rouen to South Shields in ballast. Drifted on to Holm Sand and became a total loss.

L.6 HAVRE (II)/MURISTAN (II) (1913-1916)
ON. 128946. 2886g, 1776n. 320.3 × 46.7 × 21.1 feet.
T3-cyl. by Central Marine Engine Works, West Hartlepool.
3.9.1913: Launched as HAVRE and *9.1913* completed as MURISTAN by Wm. Gray and Co. Ltd., West Hartlepool (Yard No. 831) for London & Paris Steamship Co. Ltd. *26.9.1913:* Ran trials. *19.11.1916:* Wrecked one mile South of Blyth whilst on a voyage from the River Tyne to Rouen with a cargo of coal.

Contract price £38,000 including machinery. Payable in cash on completion or £8000 in cash on delivery and the balance of £30,000 payable over 5 years in equal ½ yearly instalments plus interest at 5% per annum in advance. Security to be held in debentures in the owning company.

L.7 KING ALBERT (1914-1915)
ON. 136732. 2124g, 1288n. 281.5 × 43.1 × 19.5 feet.
T3-cyl. by North Eastern Marine Engineering Co. Ltd., Newcastle.
9.1909: Completed by Wood, Skinner and Co. Ltd., Newcastle (Yard No. 161) as BELGIQUE for Soc. Anon. Baltique (Giani & Muller managers), Belgium. *1914:* Purchased by London & Paris Steamship Co. Ltd. and renamed KING ALBERT. *8.9.1915:* Foundered 2½ miles N.W. of Ceuta after striking a submerged object in the Straits of Gibraltar whilst on a voyage from Benisaf to the River Tyne with a cargo of iron ore.

LA TUNISIENNE STEAM NAVIGATION CO. LTD.

Formed in 1910 by Frank C. Strick & Co. Ltd. and M. Jules Mesnier's Soc. Commerciale d'Affretements et de Commission, this company was to build ships specifically for the coal and iron ore trade.

In all, nineteen ships were owned by this company, employed in the carriage of coal from the U.K. to North African bunkering ports until this trade declined, and then mainly to Savona and thence to North African iron ore ports to load ore for the U.K.-Continent.

The ships were named after places in North Africa ending in 'a'. The funnel was black, having on either side the house flag motif, which was a square containing a white lozenge on which was an 'M', and the four triangular corners being alternate red and blue. The remainder of the livery was similar to the Gulf fleets. With the decline of the coal exporting trade after World War II, it was decided to close the business and the last of the vessels was sold in 1951.

Discharging coal at Oran. **CAMERATA (I)** is in the foreground *Author's Collection*

M.1 DJERISSA (1910-1927)
ON. 128910. 3723g, 2361n. 350.1 × 50.1 × 23.6 feet.
T3-cyl. by Central Marine Engine Works, West Hartlepool.
8.4.1910: Launched and *5.1910* completed by Wm. Gray and Co. Ltd., West Hartlepool (Yard No. 773) for La Tunisienne Steam Navigation Co. Ltd. *21.11.1927:* Wrecked on Newbiggin Shoal, Cresswell whilst on a voyage from Emden to the River Tyne in ballast.

Contract price £34,850 including machinery. Payable £23,350 on completion and the balance over 10 years in equal ½ yearly instalments plus interest at 4½% per annum in advance.

CAMERATA *Author's Collection*

M.2 CAMERATA (I) (1910-1929)
ON. 128912. 3723g, 2361n. 350.1 × 50.1 × 23.6 feet.
T3-cyl. by Central Marine Engine Works, West Hartlepool. Replaced in *6.1918* by a similar engine by Fullerton, Hodgart and Barclay Ltd., Paisley.
9.5.1910: Launched and *6.1910* completed by Wm. Gray and Co. Ltd., West Hartlepool (Yard No. 774) for La Tunisienne Steam Navigation Co. Ltd. *1929:* Sold to Russell — Turner Steam Ship Co. Ltd., Glasgow and renamed RONTURN. *1933:* Sold for £6000 to F. Grauds Shipping Co. Ltd., Latvia and renamed EVERARDS. *1938:* Transferred to Mrs. Z. Heinrichsons (F. Grauds manager), Latvia. *19.11.1938:* Seized by Spanish forces whilst on a voyage from the River Tyne to Oran and taken to Ceuta. *1939:* Transferred to Cia. Transmediterranea, Spain and renamed CASTILLO FUENSALDANA. *1941:* Taken over by the Spanish Government (Domingo Mumbru manager). *1942:* Transferred to Empresa Elcano de la Marina Mercante. *1955:* Sold to Jose Cru Rico, Spain. *1957:* Transferred to Naviera Cru S. A. (Jose Cru Rico manager), Spain and renamed CRU MEDITERRANEO. *1961:* Sold to Maritima Colonial y de Comercio S. A., Spain and renamed SENDYE. *18.12.1967:* Damaged by fire whilst lying at Santander. *1968:* Sold to Recuperaciones Submarinas and broken up at Santander.

Contract price £34,850 including machinery. Payable £23,350 on completion and the balance over 10 years in equal ½ yearly instalments plus interest at 4½% per annum in advance.

BOUKADRA *M. Lindenborn*

M.3 BOUKADRA (1910-1929)
ON. 128915. 3722g, 2356n. 350.1 × 50.1 × 23.6 feet.
T3-cyl. by Central Marine Engine Works, West Hartlepool.
10.6.1910: Launched and *7.1910* completed by Wm. Gray and Co. Ltd., West Hartlepool (Yard No. 776) for La Tunisienne Steam Navigation Co. Ltd. *1929:* Sold for £26,000 to Dale Steam Ship Co. Ltd. (R. Mackill and Co. managers), Glasgow and renamed YARROWDALE. *1935:* Sold for £10,000 to San Peh Steam Navigation Co. Ltd., China and renamed SUNG-SHAN. *1938:* Sold to Cia. Italiana di Nav. S.A.I. (Chinese Italian Navigation Co. Ltd.), Shanghai (Italian flag) and renamed AMBA ALAGI. *1943:* Seized by Japan and renamed AOKI MARU. *13.11.1944:* Bombed and sunk by United States carrier based aircraft off Manila in a position 14.35N, 120.55E.

Contract price £34,850 including machinery. Payable £23,350 on completion and the balance over 10 years in equal ½ yearly instalments plus interest at 4½% per annum in advance.

M.4 MOKTA (1912-1932)
ON. 128937. 3934g, 2475n. 350.0 × 50.0 × 25.3 feet.
T3-cyl. by Central Marine Engine Works, West Hartlepool.
11.10.1912: Launched and *11.1912* completed by Wm. Gray and Co. Ltd., West Hartlepool (Yard No. 815) for La Tunisienne Steam Navigation Co. Ltd. *1932:* Sold for £4500 to F. Grauds Shipping Co. Ltd., Latvia and renamed EVERALDA. *1938:* Transferred to Mrs. Z. Heinrichsons (F. Grauds manager), Latvia. *29.6.1942:* Captured S.W. of Bermuda by the German submarine U158 and sunk by gunfire in a position 31N, 70W. approx. She was on a voyage from Philadelphia for Rio de Janeiro.

Contract price £41,500 including £9950 for machinery. Payable £2000 when keel laid, £3000 when framed, £3000 when launched, £6000 on completion and the balance of £27,500 over 5 years in equal ½ yearly instalments plus interest at 5% per annum in advance. The instalments made at keel laying, framing and launching to bear interest at 4% per annum to the date of completion.

MOKTA *M. Lindenborn*

TABARKA *Author's Collection*

M.5 TABARKA (1913-1932)
ON. 128938. 3933g, 2474n. 350.0 × 50.0 × 25.3 feet.
T3-cyl. by Central Marine Engine Works, West Hartlepool.
9.12.1912: Launched and *2.1913* completed by Wm. Gray and Co. Ltd., West Hartlepool (Yard No. 817) for La Tunisienne Steam Navigation Co. Ltd. *1932:* Sold for £4500 to Antti Wihuri, Finland and renamed WIPUNEN. *12.1941:* Taken over by United States Maritime Commission, renamed GRANVILLE and placed under the Panamanian flag. *17.3.1943:* Torpedoed and sunk by the German submarine U338 in a position 52.50N, 30.35W. The ship was sailing in Convoy SC.122 at the time. of the sinking, bound from Boston and New York for Iceland with general cargo and army stores. Twelve crew were lost.

Contract price £41,400 including £9950 for machinery. Payable £2000 when keel laid, £3000 when framed, £3000 when launched, £6000 on completion and the balance of £27,400 over 5 years in equal ½ yearly instalments plus interest at 5% per annum in advance. The instalments made at keel laying, framing and launching to bear interest at 4% per annum to the date of completion.

M.6 ALGORTA (1920-1925)
ON. 142681. 3118g, 1870n. 331.3 × 46.8 × 23.2 feet.
T3-cyl. by G. Clark Ltd., Sunderland.
9.9.1918: Launched and *10.1918* completed by John Priestman and Co., Sunderland (Yard No. 266) as WAR ZEPHYR for The Shipping Controller (Herskind and Co. managers). *1919:* Sold to W. H. Vernall and Co., London and renamed ALGORTA. *1920:* Purchased by La Tunisienne Steam Navigation Co. Ltd. *1925:* Sold to Cia. Naviera Bachi (Hijos de Astigarraga manager), Spain and renamed BARTOLO. *6.3.1943:* Torpedoed and sunk by the British submarine TAURUS near Marseilles.

M.7 TUNISIA (I) (1921-1926)
ON. 142673. 3118g, 1875n. 331.2 × 46.8 × 23.2 feet.
T3-cyl. by G. Clark Ltd., Sunderland.
10.1918: Completed by Irvine's Shipbuilding and Dry Docks Co. Ltd., West Hartlepool (Yard No. 596) as WAR SIMOOM for The Shipping Controller (Hessler and Co. managers). *1919:* Sold to Swift Steamship Co. Ltd. (same managers), West Hartlepool and renamed DIBBLE BRIDGE 1921: Purchased by La Tunisienne Steam Navigation Co. Ltd and renamed TUNISIA. *1926:* Sold to Shimatani Kisen K.K., Japan and renamed AKASHI MARU. *1938:* Name rendered as AKASI MARU. *28.9.1943:* Torpedoed and sunk by the U.S. submarine BLUEFISH north of Timor Island in a position 06.11S, 126.00E.

M.8 MORA (1922-1924)
ON. 143978. 5067g, 2825n. 370.3 × 51.0 × 27.1 feet.
T3-cyl. by the shipbuilder.
7.1922: Completed by G. Seebeck A. G. Schiffswerft Maschinenfabrik und Trocken — Docks, Geestemunde (Yard No. 368) for La Tunisienne Steam Navigation Co. Ltd. *8.2.1924:* Wrecked near Cape St. Vincent whilst on a voyage from Manchester and Rotterdam to Savona with a cargo of coal.

M.9 ZEMBRA (1923-1930) (1936-1937)
ON. 143982. 5074g, 2823n. 370.5 × 51.0 × 27.1 feet.
T3-cyl by the shipbuilder.
14.8.1923: Launched and *10.1923* completed by G. Seebeck A. G. Schiffswerft Maschinenfabrik und Trocken-Docks, Geestemunde (Yard No. 369) for La Tunisienne Steam Navigation Co. Ltd. *1930:* Sold to Société Commerciale de Navigation, France. *1936:* Purchased by La Tunisienne Steam Navigation Co. Ltd. *1937:* Sold for £60,000 to Fried. Krupp A. G. (Fried. Krupp's Rederij en Transportbedrijf N. V. managers), Germany and renamed OSLEBSHAUSEN. *2.9.1941:* Torpedoed and sunk off Stavanger by British aircraft.

M.10 MEDJERDA (1924-1941)
ON. 143983. 4380g, 2719n. 370.0 × 52.0 × 25.5 feet.
T3-cyl. by Central Marine Engine Works, West Hartlepool.
19.5.1924: Launched and *6.1924* completed by Wm. Gray and Co. Ltd., West Hartlepool (Yard No. 957) for London & Paris Steamship Co. Ltd. *1924:* Transferred to La Tunisienne Steam Navigation Co. Ltd. *18.3.1941:* Torpedoed and sunk by the German submarine U105 in a position 17N, 21W. approx. whilst on a voyage from Pepel to Middlesbrough with a cargo of iron ore.

Contract price £73,000 including £19,400 for machinery. Payable $\frac{1}{5}$ on signing of contract $\frac{1}{5}$ by acceptance at 6 months from date of laying keel, $\frac{1}{5}$ in cash when steamer framed, $\frac{1}{5}$ by acceptance at 3 months from date of steamer being plated and the balance of £14,600 in cash on delivery. Cost of machinery payable $\frac{1}{5}$ when cylinders cast, $\frac{1}{5}$ when boiler shells rivetted, $\frac{1}{5}$ when cylinders bored and faced, $\frac{1}{5}$ when engine erected and boilers tested and the balance of £3880 when installation on board complete.

MEDJERDA *A. Duncan*

M.11 GOLETA (1927-1930) (1936)
ON. 143987. 2473g, 1485n. 298.5 × 43.9 × 21.2 feet.
T3-cyl. by D. Rowan and Co. Ltd., Glasgow.
3.1927: Completed by Burntisland Shipbuilding Co. Ltd., Burntisland (Yard No. 134) for La Tunisienne Steam Navigation Co. Ltd. *1930:* Sold to Société Commerciale de Navigation, France. *1936:* Purchased by La Tunisienne Steam Navigation Co. Ltd. *1936:* Sold for £29,000 to Stanhope Steamship Co. Ltd. (J. A. Billmeir and Co. Ltd. managers), London and renamed STANHOLME. *25.12.1939:* Mined and sunk in the Bristol Channel in a position 51.20N, 03.39W. She was on a voyage from Cardiff for London with 4500 tons of coal. Thirteen crew were lost.

GOLETA *G. Scott Collection*

M.12 TUNISIA (II) (1927-1941)
ON. 143988. 4337g, 2693n. 370.2 × 52.3 × 25.9 feet.
T3-cyl. by the shipbuilder.
30.4.1927: Launched and *6.1927* completed by J. Readhead and Sons Ltd., South Shields (Yard No. 483) for La Tunisienne Steam Navigation Co. Ltd. *2.6.1927:* Ran trials. *4.8.1941:* Bombed and sunk by German aircraft in a position 53.53N, 18.10W. The crew took to the boats but 38 men were lost. There were only five survivors, including the master, Captain W. A. Shute, O.B.E. She was on a voyage from Pepel for Workington with 6500 tons of manganese and iron ore.

TUNISIA *South Tyneside Museum*

GUELMA on trials *South Tyneside Museum*

M.13 GUELMA (1928-1941)
ON. 143989. 4402g, 2738n. 370.2 × 52.3 × 25.9 feet.
T3-cyl. by the shipbuilder.
23.2.1928: Launched and *3.1928* completed by J. Readhead and Sons Ltd., South Shields (Yard No. 489) for La Tunisienne Steam Navigation Co. Ltd. *30.3.1928:* Ran trials. *17.7.1941:* Torpedoed and sunk by the Italian submarine ALLESANDRO MALASPINA in a position 30.44N, 17.33W. She was on a voyage from Madeira for Pepel with general cargo.

M.14 BRIKA (1929-1950)
ON. 143998. 4412g, 2736n. 370.6 × 52.3 × 25.9 feet.
T3-cyl. by the shipbuilder.
26.3.1929: Launched and *5.1929* completed by J. Readhead and Sons Ltd., South Shields (Yard No. 495) for La Tunisienne Steam Navigation Co. Ltd. *1.5.1929:* Ran trials. *1950:* Sold to Wheelock, Marden and Co. Ltd., Hong Kong. *1951:* Sold to Inui Kisen K. K., Japan and renamed KENZUI MARU. *1958:* Sold to Hokusei Kaiun K. K., Japan and renamed SORACHI MARU. *1965:* Sold to Japanese shipbreakers and *26.2.1965* demolition commenced at Hirao.

TAFNA *W.S.P.L.*

M.15 TAFNA (1930-1939)
ON. 144000. 4413g, 2738n. 370.3 × 52.3 × 25.9 feet.
T3-cyl. by the shipbuilder.
15.3.1930: Launched and *4.1930* completed by J. Readhead and Sons Ltd., South Shields (Yard No. 501) for La Tunisienne Steam Navigation Co. Ltd. *30.4.1930:* Ran trials. *24.10.1939:* Torpedoed and sunk by the German submarine U37 in a position 35.44N, 07.23W. She was on a voyage from Benisaf for London with 6900 tons of iron ore. Two crew were lost.

TAFNA *W.S.P.L.*

CAMERATA *F. Hawks*

M.16 CAMERATA (II) (1931-1943)
ON. 144002. 4840g, 3006n. 393.4 × 53.8 × 26.6 feet.
T3-cyl. by the shipbuilder. Replaced in *1951* by a similar engine by General Machinery Corporation, Hamilton, Ohio.
4.12.1930: Launched and *5.1931* completed by J. Readhead and Sons Ltd., South Shields (Yard No. 505) for La Tunisienne Steam Navigation Co. Ltd. *12.5.1931:* Ran trials. *8.5.1943:* Sunk at Gibraltar by Italian assault craft and declared a constructive total loss. *1946:* Sold to Compania Naviera de Transportes y Pesca S. A., Spain. *1950:* Renamed CAMPO GRANDE and in *1951* returned to service. *1965:* Sold to Riva Suardiaz, Angel & Others, Spain. *4.4.1971:* Sank in a position 26.18N, 16.34W. after fire had broken out the previous day when she was about 100 miles south of Las Palmas whilst on a voyage from Santander to Duala in ballast.

M.17 ZEMBRA (1936-1937)
See ZEMBRA (No. M.9)

M.18 GOLETA (1936)
See GOLETA (No. M.11)

KERMA *G. Scott Collection*

M.19 KERMA (1943-1951)
See KERMA (No. N.1)

M.20 CAMERATA (III) (1947-1951)
ON. 149451. 5573g; 3353n. 395.5 × 54.0 × 29.1 feet.
T3-cyl by MacColl and Pollock Ltd., Sunderland.
13.8.1927: Launched and *3.1928* completed by Bartram and Sons Ltd., Sunderland (Yard No. 260) as BADJESTAN for Hindustan Steam Shipping Co. Ltd. (Common Brothers managers), Newcastle. *1946:* Sold to Quayside Shipping Co. Ltd. (Wm. Brown, Atkinson and Co. Ltd. managers), Hull and renamed FERRIBY. *1947:* Purchased by La Tunisienne Steam Navigation Co. Ltd. and renamed CAMERATA. *1951:* Sold for £225,000 to Cia. Nacional Nav. S. A., Panama and renamed MARIA. *1955:* Sold for £180,000 to Compania Maritima Somalegra S.A., Panama and renamed SOMALEGRA. *27.1.1960:* Arrived at Aviles to be broken up by Desquaces y Salvamentos del Nervion.

CAMERATA as **SOMALEGRA** *Skyfotos*

M.21 LEON DE NERVO (1948-1951)

ON. 147722. 4991g, 3038n. 396.6 × 53.1 × 26.5 feet.
T3-cyl. by the shipbuilder.
14.8.1924: Launched and *9.1924* completed by Workman, Clark and Co. Ltd., Belfast (Yard No. 470) as BARRINGTON COURT for Court Line Ltd. (Haldin and Co. Ltd. managers), London. *1929:* Transferred to United British Steamship Co. Ltd. (Haldin and Philipps Ltd. managers). *1936:* Owners name changed to Court Line Ltd. (same managers). *1946:* Transferred to United British Steamship Co. Ltd. (same managers). *1948:* Purchased by La Tunisienne Steam Navigation Co. Ltd. and renamed LEON DE NERVO. *1951:* Sold for £140,000 to Cia. Puerto Rico S.A. (V. Tricoglou manager), Panama and renamed ELETRIC. *13.8.1960:* Stranded one mile N.W. of Ras al Jidufa, Masirah Island after developing a leak and abandoned as a total loss. She was on a voyage from Mormugao to Lubeck with a cargo of iron ore.

LEON DE NERVO as **BARRINGTON COURT** *W.S.P.L.*

CORY & STRICK (STEAMERS) LTD.

This company was formed in 1928 by Frank C. Strick & Co. Ltd. and William Cory & Sons Ltd. It built ships to run in conjunction with La Tunisienne Steam Navigation Co. Ltd., in the coal and iron ore trade, under the management of Frank C. Strick and Co. Ltd. Six ships were built between 1928 and 1931, but then the depression put an end to the programme and no more ships were built for this fleet. In 1943, with only three ships remaining, it was decided to wind up the business and the ships were sold.

Names of the ships were similar to those of La Tunisienne Steam Navigation Co. Ltd., the livery was similar also, except that the funnel and flag device had the Cory black diamond in place of the white diamond and 'M'.

KERMA *Author's Collection*

N.1 KERMA (1928-1943)
ON. 160568. 4333g, 2658n. 370.0 × 52.2 × 25.9 feet.
T3-cyl. by the shipbuilder.
21.8.1928: Launched and *9.1928* completed by D. and W. Henderson and Co. Ltd., Glasgow (Yard No. 813) for Cory and Strick (Steamers) Ltd. *1943:* Transferred to La Tunisienne Steam Navigation Co. Ltd. *1951:* Sold for £140,000 to Nya Angfartygs A/B Heimdal (Rudolf Hellberg manager), Sweden and renamed HEIMDAL. *4.3.1957:* Stranded in fog at Stangskar Point, Landsort after developing a leak whilst on a voyage from the River Tyne to Oxelosund with a cargo of cars, tractors and general cargo. *19.3.1957:* Broke in two and the after part sank. *13.9.1957:* Fore part sank during a storm.

N.2 BATNA (1928-1942)
ON. 160569. 4399g, 2735n. 370.0 × 52.3 × 25.9 feet.
T3-cyl. by the shipbuilder.
16.8.1928: Launched and *9.1928* completed by J. Readhead and Sons Ltd., South Shields (Yard No. 492) for Cory and Strick (Steamers) Ltd. *20.9.1928:* Ran trials. *13.5.1942:* Torpedoed and sunk by the German submarine U94 in a position 52,09N, 33.56W. whilst on a voyage from Newport, Mon. to Halifax, N.S. with 4988 tons of coal.

N.3 MARSA (1928-1943)
ON. 160601. 4405g, 2738n. 370.0 × 52.3 × 25.9 feet.
T3-cyl. by the shipbuilder.
29.9.1928: Launched and *11.1928* completed by J. Readhead and Sons Ltd., South Shields (Yard No. 493) for Cory and Strick (Steamers) Ltd. *3.11.1928:* Ran trials. *1943:* Sold to United British Steamship Co. Ltd. (Haldin and Philipps Ltd. managers), London. *21.11.1943:* Bombed by German aircraft in a position 46.40N, 18.18W. when on a voyage from Oran and Gibraltar for Ardrossan with 6230 tons of iron ore. She was last seen afloat *22.11.1943* in position 46.35N. 18.20W.

MARSA *South Tyneside Museum*

THALA *A. Duncan*

N.4 THALA (1928-1941)
ON. 160623. 4399g, 2736n. 370.0 × 52.3 × 25.9 feet.
T3-cyl. by the shipbuilder.
14.11.1928: Launched and *12.1928* completed by J. Readhead and Sons Ltd., South Shields (Yard No. 494) for Cory and Strick (Steamers) Ltd. *20.12.1928:* Ran trials.
8.2.1941: Wrecked at Hartimeal, Eriskay Sound, South Uist, Outer Hebrides whilst on a voyage from Pepel to the River Tees with a cargo of iron ore.

HAMLA on trials *South Tyneside Museum*

N.5 HAMLA (1929-1942)
ON. 161290. 4416g, 2737n. 370.4 × 52.3 × 25.9 feet.
T3-cyl. by the shipbuilder.
25.7.1929: Launched and *8.1929* completed by J. Readhead and Sons Ltd., South Shields (Yard No. 497) for Cory and Strick (Steamers) Ltd. *31.8.1929:* Ran trials. *11.8.1942:* Sailed from Rio de Janeiro bound for Freetown with a crew of 38 men and four gunners. *23.8.1942:* Torpedoed and sunk by the German submarine U506 in a position 4 S, 24 W. approx. There were no survivors.

LORCA *A. Duncan*

N.6 LORCA (1931-1943)
ON. 162525, 4875g, 3007n. 393.4 × 53.8 × 26.6 feet.
T3-cyl. by the shipbuilder.
22.9.1930: Launched and *1.1931* completed by J. Readhead and Sons Ltd., South Shields (Yard No. 504) for Cory and Strick (Steamers) Ltd. *12.1.1931:* Ran trials. *1943:* Sold to United British Steamship Co. Ltd. (Haldin and Philipps Ltd managers), London. *1944:* Sold to Maritime Shipping and Trading Co. Ltd. (Michalinos and Co. Ltd. managers), London. *1946:* Renamed LORADORE. *13.8.1955:* Stranded off Bird Rocks, Magdalen Island, Gulf of St. Lawrence during fog whilst on a voyage from Sydney N.S. to Montreal with a cargo of coal. *17.8.1955:* Abandoned when the vessel began to break up.

NORTH DEVON STEAMSHIP CO. LTD.

When, in 1922, Mr. Strick bought a ship for himself unconnected with all his other businesses, he formed North Devon Steamship Co. Ltd. to operate her. This name, and the name he gave to the ship, reflected his love of that part of the country where for many years he had a country home, above Lynmouth, overlooking the Bristol Channel. His ship had a black funnel with a blue band on which was a white 'S', but this livery was not destined to become famous and it is doubtful if anyone now remembers it. The ship was sold after little more than a year and, although the company remained in existence, no more ships were bought for it. In 1942 the company became Frank C. Strick & Co. (S. Wales) Ltd., operating in conjunction with Strick, Gorchs Ltd. at Cardiff.

EXMOOR *W.S.P.L.*

P.1 WEST CARUTH/EXMOOR (1922-1924)
ON. 146651. 5689g, 4029n. 410.5 × 54.3 × 27.2 feet.
T3-cyl. by Llewellyn Iron Works, Los Angeles.
1919: Completed by South Western Shipbuilding Co., San Pedro, California (Yard No. 2) as WEST CARUTH for the United States Shipping Board. *1922:* Purchased by North Devon Steamship Co. Ltd. *1923:* Renamed EXMOOR. *1924:* Sold to D. Tripcovich, Italy and renamed ANTONIO TRIPCOVICH. *1928:* Sold for £51,500 to Oguma Shoten Gomei Kaisha, Japan and renamed SEISHO MARU. *1938:* Name rendered as SEISYO MARU. *18.11.1944:* Torpedoed and sunk by the U.S. submarine SUNFISH in a position 33.36N, 124.18E.

SHIPS MANAGED ON BEHALF OF THE GOVERNMENT AND OTHER OWNERS

KERMAN *Author's Collection*

Q.1 KERMAN (1915-1916)
ON. 136777, 4397g, 2758n 389.0 × 51.0 × 25.2 feet.
T3-cyl. by the shipbuilder.
20.7.1907: Launched and *8.1907* completed by Flensburger Schiffsbau Gesellschaft, Flensburg (Yard No. 273) as FURTH for Deutsch Austalische Dampfschiffs-Gesellschaft, Germany. *10.8.1914:* Captured off Ceylon by H.M.S. ESPIEGLE whilst on a voyage from Sydney to Suez. *11.8.1914:* Arrived at Colombo and *5.10.1914* condemned as a prize. *1915:* Sold to Anglo-Persian Oil Co. Ltd., London and renamed KERMAN. *1915:* Transferred to British Tanker Co. Ltd., London and placed under the management of F. C. Strick and Co. Ltd., *1916:* Management ceased. *1920:* Sold to Persian Gulf Steam Navigation Co. Ltd., Bombay and renamed SULTANIA. *1930:* Sold to Bengal Burma Steam Navigation Co. Ltd. (A. B. Chowdry manager), Rangoon. *1933:* Sold to shipbreakers at Bombay.

Q.2 SENEGAMBIA (1915-1916)
ON. 137685.. 3780g. 2387n. 371.2 × 44.2 × 27.1 feet.
T.3-cyl. by the shipbuilder.
3.4.1895: Launched and *5.1895* completed by Blohm & Voss, Hamburg (Yard No. 107) as BELLONA for Deutsche Dampfschiffs-Rhederei zu Hamburg, Germany. *1898:* Sold to Norddeutscher Lloyd Germany and renamed NURNBERG. *1904:* Sold to Hamburg-Amerikanische Packetfahrt A.G., Germany and renamed SENEGAMBIA. *21.8.1914:* Captured near Tsingtao by H.M.S. TRIUMPH and the French cruiser DUPLEIX whilst on a voyage from Hamburg and Rotterdam to Yokohama and taken to Hong Kong. *1915:* Requisitioned by the British Government and placed under the management of F. C Strick and Co. Ltd. *1916:* Transferred to France, allocated to Cie. Generale Transatlantique and renamed LAMENTIN. *1925:* Sold to Italian shipbreakers.

SENEGAMBIA as **NURNBERG** *W.S.P.L.*

Q.3 HUNTSGULF (1917-1919)
ON. 99075. 3185g, 2034n. 325.9 × 40.2 × 19.1 feet.
T.3-cyl. by Wallsend Slipway Co. Ltd., Wallsend.
14.3.1892: Launched and *5.1892* completed by Edwards' Shipbuilding Co. Ltd., Newcastle (Yard No. 59) as BRANKSOME TOWER for F. Stumore and Co. Ltd., London. *1892:* Sold to Hamburg-Sudamerikanische D.G., Germany and renamed RIO. *3.1.1902:* Sold to Deutsche Levante Linie, Germany and renamed SERIPHOS. *8.1914:* Interned at Piraeus. *3.9.1916:* Seized by the Allies and *30.10.1916* arrived at Malta for repairs. *1917:* Allocated to The Shipping Controller (F. C. Strick and Co. Ltd., managers) and renamd HUNTSGULF. *1919:* Sold to P. Mitrovich, Yugoslavia and renamed JUGOSLAVEN PRVI. *1924:* Sold to Josip Ucovic, Yugoslavia and renamed VOJSLAV. *1927:* Sold to T. W. Ward Ltd. and broken up at Inverkeithing.

Q.4 ANNE (1918-1922)
ON. 139029. 4083g, 2572n. 367.1 × 47.7 × 27.3 feet.
T.3-cyl. by Bremer Vulkan Schiffbau & Maschinenfabrik, Vegesack.
16.2.1911: Launched and *3.1911* completed by Rickmers Reismuhlen Rhederei und Schiffbau A.G., Geestemunde (Yard No. 159) as AENNE RICKMERS for their own account. *8.1914:* Seized at Port Said whilst on a voyage from Yokohama to Hamburg and requisitioned by the Admiralty. *4.8.1915:* Commissioned in the Royal Navy and renamed H.M.S. ANNE. Converted into a seaplane carrier carrying two seaplanes and served in the Eastern Mediterranean. *8.8.1917:* Decommissioned and later served as a store carrier. *1.1918:* Transferred to The Shipping Controller (F. C. Strick and Co. Ltd., managers). *1922:* Sold to Stylianos N. Vlassopulos, Greece and renamed ITHAKI. *1939:* Sold to Spiridion N. Vlassopol, Roumania and renamed MOLDOVA. *1941:* Transferred to the Panamanian flag and registered in the ownership of Cia. Ithaca de Vapores S.A. *1949:* Sold to Wallem and Co. Ltd., Panama. *1954:* Renamed JAGRAHAT. *1955:* Renamed MOLDOVA. *8.11.1958:* Arrived at Hong Kong to be broken up by Patt Manfield & Co. Ltd.

Q.5 MAASHAVEN (1918-1919)
ON. 142728. 2609g, 1689n. 305.0 × 44.6 × 21.0 feet.
T3-cyl. by Maatschappij de Schelde, Flushing.
1906: Completed by Bonn & Mees, Rotterdam (Yard No. 177) as MAASHAVEN for N.V. Maatschappij S.S. Maashaven (Gebr. Van Uden, managers), Netherlands. *1918:* Taken over by The Shipping Controller (F. C. Strick and Co. Ltd., managers). *1919:* Returned to owners, *1925:* Managers restyled as N. V. Gebr. Van Uden's Scheepvaart en Agentuur Maatschappij. *1940:* Sold to Wm. H. Muller & Co. N.V. and Koninklijke Nederlandsche Hoogovens en Staalfabrieken N.V., Netherlands and renamed ZUIJDERBURGH. *1947:* Sold to Rederi A/B Fanny (Algot Johansson, manager), Finland and renamed FANNY. *1953:* Registered in the ownership of Rederi A/B Sally following a merger of Rederi A/B Fanny with this company. *30.10.1959:* Arrived in tow at Rotterdam to be broken up by Metaalhandel & Sloopw. Heuvelman at Krimpen a/d Yssel.

Q.6 HERSFELD (1919-1921)
ON. 143223. 4487g, 2855n. 389.7 × 48.0 × 28.2 feet.
T.3-cyl. by the shipbuilder.
4.6.1897: Launched and *7.1897* completed by Flensburger Schiffsbau Gesellschaft, Flensburg (Yard No. 167) as MEISSEN for Deutsch-Australische Dampfschiffs-Gesellschaft, Germany. *1913:* Sold to Rhederei Akt. Ges. 'Oceana' (H. H. Schmidt, manager), Germany and renamed WOGLINDE. *1917:* Sold to Continentale Rhederei Akt. Ges., Germany and renamed HERSFELD. *1919:* Surrendered to Great Britain as a prize and allocated to The Shipping Controller (F. C. Strick and Co. Ltd., managers). *1921:* Sold to H. Kayser & Sohn G.m.b.H., Germany and renamed RUTH KAYSER. *1923:* Registered in the ownership of Reederei Kayser A.G. *1926:* Sold to P. and W. MacLellan Ltd. for £7,000 and broken up at Bo'ness.

Q.7 LENNEP (1919-1920)
ON. 143385. 4972g, 3038n. 419.9 × 54.1 × 26.3 feet.
T3-cyl. by the shipbuilder.
11.1915: Launched by A. G. 'Neptun', Rostock (Yard No. 344) as MULHAUSEN for Deutsche Australische Dampfschiffs-Gesellschaft, Germany. *1.1919:* Completed as LENNEP for Deutsche Dampfschifffahrts Gesellschaft 'Kosmos', Germany. *1919:* Surrendered to Great Britain as a prize and allocated to The Shipping Controller (F. C. Strick and Co. Ltd., managers). *1920:* Sold to J. Coull and Sons, Newcastle and renamed BRANT COUNTY. *1921:* Sold to Det Bergenske D/S., Norway. *11.3.1943:* Torpedoed and sunk by the German submarine U.757 in a position 52.05N, 27.35W whilst on a voyage from Halifax, N.S. to Liverpool.

Q.8 SCHWABEN (1919-1921)
ON. 143204. 5098g, 3225n. 410.4 × 52.7 × 28.0 feet.
Q4-cyl. by the shipbuilder.
5.2.1906: Launched and *3.1906* completed by Bremer Vulkan, Vegesack (Yard No. 484) as SCHWABEN for Norddeutscher Lloyd, Germany. *8.1914:* Refitted as an artillery transport at Bremerhaven. *1917:* Employed as an auxiliary hospital ship and later as a repair ship at Wilhelmshaven. *1919:* Surrendered to Great Britain as a prize and allocated to The Shipping Controller (F. C. Strick and Co. Ltd., managers). *30.6.1921:* Sold to Cornborough Shipping Co. Ltd. (Sir William Reardon Smith and Sons (London) Ltd., managers), Cardiff and renamed CRAGNESS. *1924:* Transferred to Oakwin Steamship Co. Ltd. (Sir William Reardon Smith and Sons Ltd., managers). *30.4.1924:* Wrecked 40 miles south of Mozambique whilst on a voyage from Port Natal to Perim with a cargo of coal.

Q.9 WALDENBURG (1919-1921)
ON. 143140. 5826g, 3627n. 450.0 × 58.1 × 26.9 feet.
T3-cyl. by the shipbuilder.
16.8.1916: Launched and *6.1917* completed by Flensburger Schiffsbau Gesellschaft, Flensburg (Yard No. 347) as WALDENBURG for Deutsche Australische Dampfschiffs-Geselschaft, Germany. *1919:* Surrendered to Great Britain as a prize and allocated to The Shipping Controller (F. C. Strick and Co. Ltd., managers). *17.3.1921:* Sold to William Thomas Shipping Co. Ltd. (R. J. Thomas and Co., managers), Holyhead and renamed MARITIME. *1922:* Renamed CAMBRIAN QUEEN. *1928:* Sold to Norddeutscher Lloyd, Germany and renamed REMSCHEID. *1932:* Sold to the U.S.S.R. and renamed KIEV. *13.4.1942:* Torpedoed and sunk by the German submarine U.435 in a position 73.22N, 28.48E.

Q.10 CARSO/EMPIRE TANA (1941-1944)
ON. 159360. 6275g, 3955n. 419.0 × 54.0 × 30.1 feet.
T3-cyl. by United Machine Factories, Smichow.
23.9.1922: Launched and *1.1923* completed by Stabilimento Tecnico Triestino, Trieste (Yard No. 737) as CARSO for Navigazione Triestina Soc. in Azioni, Italy. *1937:* Taken over by Lloyd Triestino Soc. Anon. di Navigazione, Italy. *12.2.1941:* Scuttled at Kismayu, Italian Somaliland. Subsequently salved and after repair allocated to Ministry of War Transport (F. C. Strick and Co. Ltd., managers). *1943:* Renamed EMPIRE TANA. *1944:* Management transferred to J. and J. Denholm Ltd. *9.6.1944:* Scuttled as a blockship in Gooseberry No. 5, Mulberry Harbour, Ouistrehamn, Normandy. *1947:* Raised and towed to Strangford Lough, Northern Ireland and broken up.

CARSO *W.S.P.L.*

Q.11 EMPIRE CAMERON (1941-1943)
ON. 168704. 7015g, 5174n. 432.2 × 56.3 × 34.2 feet.
T3-cyl. by J. G. Kincaid and Co. Ltd., Greenock.
19.11.1941: Launched and *12.1941* completed by William Denny and Bros. Ltd., Dumbarton (Yard No. 1358) for Ministry of War Transport (F. C. Strick and Co. Ltd., managers). *1943:* Management transferred to Shakespear Shipping Co. Ltd. *1946:* Purchased by Shakespear Shipping Co. Ltd. (South American Saint Line Ltd., managers), Cardiff and renamed ST. MARGARET. *1951:* Transferred to South American Saint Line Ltd. *1960:* Sold to Agna Cia. Naviera S.A., Lebanon and renamed AGNA. *1963:* Sold to Japanese shipbreakers and *16.7.1963:* arrived at Yawata. Subsequently moved to Hirao where demolition commenced *15.11.1963.*

EMPIRE CAMERON as **ST. MARGARET** *W.S.P.L.*

Q.12 OCEAN SEAMAN (1942-1943)
ON. 168839. 7178g, 4280n. 425.6 × 57.0 × 34.8 feet.
T3-cyl. by Canadian Allis-Chalmers Ltd., Montreal.
16.8.1942: Launched and *9.1942* completed by Todd-Bath Iron Shipbuilding Corporation, Portland, Maine (Yard No. 22) for Ministry of War Transport (F. C. Strick and Co. Ltd., managers). *15.3.1943:* Torpedoed and sunk by the German submarine U.380 in a position 36.55N, 01.59E whilst on a voyage from Philippeville and Algiers to Gibraltar and Liverpool in ballast.

FORT POPLAR as **ETRUSCO** ashore in 1956 *W.S.P.L.*

Q.13 FORT POPLAR (1942-1947)
ON. 168385. 7134g, 4244n. 424.6 × 57.2 × 34.9 feet.
T3-cyl. by Dominion Engineering Works Ltd., Montreal.
12.9.1942: Launched and *11.1942* completed by Burrard Dry Dock Co. Ltd., Vancouver (Yard No. 149) for United States War Shipping Administration and bareboat chartered to Ministry of War Transport (F. C. Strick and Co. Ltd., managers). *1947:* Returned to United States Maritime Commission, *1948:* Sold to L'Italica di Navigazione S.A. (M. Querci, manager), Italy and renamed ETRUSCO. *16.3.1956:* Stranded in bad weather near Cedar Point, Scituate, Mass. whilst on a voyage from Emden to Boston and abandoned to the insurance underwriters. *22.11.1956:* Refloated and taken in tow to Boston for examination. *25.12.1956:* Left Boston in tow for Baltimore having been sold to Victor Transport Corp., Liberia. *1957:* Returned to service after repair and renamed SCITUATE. *1961:* Sold to Blessing Soc. Anon., Greece and renamed IRENE X. *8.4.1964:* Stranded off Haiphong in a position 20.37N, 107.12E whilst on a voyage from Haiphong to Korea with a cargo of apatite ore. *11.4.1964:* Refloated in a badly damaged condition and declared a total loss. *10.5.1964:* Arrived in tow at Hong Kong to be broken up. *9.8.1964:* Broke from her moorings during a typhoon and suffered further damage before breaking up commenced.

Q.14 FORT HOWE (1942-1943)
ON. 168395. 7133g, 4244n. 424.6 × 57.2 × 34.9 feet.
T3-cyl. by Canadian Allis-Chalmers Ltd., Montreal.
13.10.1942: Launched and *11.1942* completed by Burrard Dry Dock Co. Ltd., Vancouver (Yard No. 166) for United States War Shipping Administration and bareboat chartered to Ministry of War Transport (F. C. Strick and Co. Ltd., managers). *30.9.1943:* Torpedoed and sunk by the German submarine U.410 in a position 37.19N, 06.40E whilst on a voyage from Salerno to the United Kingdom in ballast.

Q.15 FORT LAWRENCE (1943-1948)
ON. 169883. 7134g, 4244n. 424.6 × 57.2 × 34.9 feet.
T3-cyl. by Dominion Engineering Works Ltd., Montreal.
23.11.1942: Launched and *1.1943* completed by Burrard Dry Dock Co. Ltd., Vancouver (Yard No. 155) for United States War Shipping Administration and bareboat chartered to Ministry of War Transport (F. C. Strick and Co. Ltd., managers). *1948:* Returned to United States Maritime Commission, *1958:* Sold to Pinto Island Metal Co., Mobile, Alabama and broken up.

Q,16 EMPIRE CANYON (1943-1946)
ON. 166216. 7058g, 4871n. 431.3 × 56.3 × 35.2 feet.
T3-cyl. by North Eastern Marine Engineering Co. (1938] Ltd., Newcastle.
11.11.1943: Launched and *12.1943* completed by Caledon Shipbuilding and Engineering Co. Ltd., Dundee (Yard No. 408) for Ministry of War Transport (F. C. Strick and Co. Ltd., managers). *1946:* Sold for £128,000 to Alexander Shipping Co. Ltd. (Capper, Alexander and Co., managers), London. *1947:* Renamed HOLMBURY. *1947:* Managment transferred to Houlder Bros. and Co. Ltd. *1960:* Sold for £95,000 to United Oriental Steamship Co., Pakistan and renamed ILYABAKSH. *12.4.1965:* Detained at Bombay on the outbreak of war between India and Pakistan and placed under arrest in *11.1966. 1970:* Sold to Najabali & Co. who commenced breaking up at Bombay in *10.1970.*

Q.17 EMPIRE STUART (1944-1946)
ON. 180127. 7067g, 4879n. 431.0 × 56.3 × 35.2 feet.
T3-cyl. by North Eastern Marine Engineering Co. (1938) Ltd., Newcastle upon Tyne.
29.10.1943: Launched and *2.1944* completed by Short Bros. Ltd., Sunderland (Yard No. 479) for Ministry of War Transport (F. C. Strick and Co. Ltd., managers). *11.11.1946:* Sold to Norwood Steamship Co. Ltd., (Ships Finance and Management Co. Ltd., managers), London. *1947:* Renamed LORD LLOYD GEORGE. *1955:* Sold for £260,000 to N. V. Rotterdamsche Kolen Centrale (Rotterdamsche Kustvaart Centrale N. V., managers), Netherlands and renamed ATJE-RAY-S. *1957:*Sold to Insulare Cia. Sicula di Armamento, Italy and renamed GIANFRANCO. *1964:* Sold to Italian shipbreakers and broken up at Vado.

Q.18 EL FLAMINGO (1965-1970)
ON. 183298. 6138g, 3335n. 406.0 × 56.2 × 30.0 feet.
3-cyl. 2 S.C.S.A. oil engine by the shipbuilder.
2.2.1950: Launched and *7.1950* completed by Wm. Doxford and Sons Ltd., Sunderland (Yard No. 779) as BRITISH DEFENDER for British Tanker Co. Ltd., London. *1965:* Purchased by Trustee Secretaries Ltd. (F. C. Strick and Co. (Newcastle) Ltd., managers), London and renamed EL FLAMINGO. *1969:* Conversion to a self unloading hopper dredger completed. *1970:* Sold to J. Murphy and Sons Ltd., London. *1970:* Sold to Transworld Marine Trailers Inc., Liberia. *1972:* Sold to Marcon R.M.C. Ltd. (J. Murphy and Sons Ltd., managers), London. *2.2.1982:* Sold to Belcon Shipping and Trading Co. Ltd., London and resold to Bruges Scheepslopperij to be broken up at Bruges where she arrived from London in tow *10.2.1982.*

APPENDIX "A"

Vessels built for Strick companies by William Gray & Co. Ltd., West Hartlepool.

Name	Yard No	Completed	Remarks
Baluchistan (I)	510	February 1896	Sold 1899
Laristan	526	December 1896	Sank after collision 1899
Afghanistan (I)	531	February 1897	Lost by stranding 1904
Koordistan	548	March 1898	Sold 1906
Goolistan	549	April 1898	Sank after collision 1904
Turkistan (II)	566	December 1898	Sold 1904
Bardistan (I)	574	March 1899	Sold 1899
Gorjistan (I)	613	September 1900	Sold 1904
Tabaristan (I)	620	November 1900	Sold 1902
Armanistan (I)	627	January 1901	Sold 1901
Tabaristan (II)	676	November 1903	Sold 1906
Luristan (I)	677	January 1904	Sold 1905
Turkistan (III)	698	March 1905	Sold 1910
Gorjistan (II)	699	May 1905	Sold 1910
Havre (I)	713	September 1905	Sold 1912
Tangistan (I)	736	October 1906	War loss 1915
Djerissa	773	May 1910	Wrecked 1927
Camerata (I)	774	June 1910	Sold 1929
Boukadra	776	July 1910	Sold 1929
Baltistan (I)	777	June 1910	Sold 1912
Registan (II)	778	July 1910	Sold 1911
Armanistan (III)	786	February 1911	Sold 1912
Gorjistan (III)	794	August 1911	Sold 1913
Turkistan (IV)	797	November 1911	Sold 1913
Arabistan (III)	802	May 1912	Sold 1913
Sharistan	805	July 1912	Sold on completion
	811	November 1912	Sold before completion
Baharistan (I)	814	September 1912	Sold 1914
Mokta	815	November 1912	Sold 1932
	816	February 1913	Sold before completion
Tabarka	817	February 1913	Sold 1932
	819	March 1913	Sold before completion
	820	May 1913	Sold before completion
Shahristan (IV)	822	April 1913	Sold before completion
Arabistan (IV)	827	August 1913	Sold 1913
Muristan (II)	831	September 1913	Wrecked 1916
Shahristan (V)	830	November 1913	Sold before completion
Nigaristan (III)	835	November 1913	Sold 1918
	888	November 1917	Sold before completion
Kara (II)	926	October 1919	Wrecked 1920
	943	October 1921	Sold before completion
	948	July 1922	Sold before completion
Bardistan (V)	951	April 1923	Sold 1928
Kohistan (II)	952	June 1923	Sold 1928
Medjerda	957	June 1924	War loss 1941
Arabistan (VII)	982	April 1927	War loss 1943

This list excludes vessels purchased by Strick companies from other owners.

APPENDIX "B"

Vessels built for Strick companies by John Readhead & Sons Ltd. at South Shields.

Name	Yard No	Completed	Remarks
Arabistan (VI)	482	November 1926	Sold before completion
Tunisia (II)	483	June 1927	War loss 1941
Guelma	489	March 1928	War loss 1941
Baharistan (II)	490	June 1928	Broken up 1960
Floristan (I)	491	August 1928	Wrecked 1942
Batna	492	September 1928	War loss 1942
Marsa	493	November 1928	Sold 1943
Thala	494	December 1928	Wrecked 1941
Brika	495	May 1929	Sold 1950
Arabistan (VIII)	496	August 1929	War loss 1942
Hamla	497	August 1929	War loss 1942
Gorjistan (IV)	498	November 1929	Broken up 1960
Kohistan (III)	499	January 1930	Broken up 1959
Registan (IV)	500	March 1930	War loss 1942
Tafna	501	April 1930	War loss 1939
Lorca	504	January 1931	Sold 1943
Camerata (II)	505	May 1931	War loss 1943
Armanistan (IV)	507	January 1937	War loss 1940
Baltistan (II)	508	May 1937	War loss 1941
Shahristan (VIII)	513	September 1938	War loss 1941
Turkistan (VI)	514	January 1939	Sold 1961
Afghanistan (III)	516	March 1940	Sold 1962
Baluchistan (III)	517	June 1940	War loss 1942
Shahristan (IX)	544	April 1945	Broken up 1962
Nigaristan (V)	551	March 1947	Sold 1967
Tabaristan (VI)	553	June 1947	Sold 1968
Registan (VI)	555	December 1947	Sold 1964
Armanistan (V)	561	April 1949	Sold 1965
Goulistan	563	April 1950	Broken up 1962
Tangistan (II)	567	June 1950	Broken up 1972
Muristan (IV)	566	October 1950	Sold 1966
Baltistan (III)	573	July 1953	To P & O 1972
Khuzistan	580	January 1955	To P & O 1972
Baluchistan (IV)	585	May 1956	To P & O 1972
Seistan (II)	592	July 1957	Lost by explosion 1958
Karaghistan	593	November 1957	To P & O 1972
Farsistan (II)	599	May 1959	To P & O 1972
Kohistan (IV)	605	November 1960	To P & O 1972
Gorjistan (V)	608	November 1961	To P & O 1972
Turkistan (VII)	611	January 1963	To P & O 1972
Shahristan (X)	614	January 1965	To P & O 1972
Floristan (III)	615	June 1965	To P & O 1972
Serbistan (IV)	617	March 1966	To P & O 1972
Registan (VII)	618	August 1966	To P & O 1972

and built at Readheads yard by Swan, Hunter Shipbuilders Ltd.

Tabaristan (VII)	9	May 1969	To P & O 1972
Nigaristan (VI)	32	November 1970	To P & O 1972

APPENDIX "C"

Wartime losses by enemy action.

Name	Built	Date lost	How lost
Tangistan (I)	1906	9-3-1915	Submarine — torpedo.
Kara (I)	1889	10-7-1916	Mined.
Avristan (II)	1901	7-12-1916	Submarine — torpedo.
Huntstrick	1902	8-6-1917	Submarine — torpedo.
Seistan (I)	1907	23-10-1917	Submarine — torpedo.
Kohistan (I)	1908	22-11-1917	Submarine — torpedo.
Tafna	1930	24-10-1939	Submarine — torpedo.
Armanistan (IV)	1937	3-2-1940	Submarine — torpedo.
Baltistan (II)	1937	27-2-1941	Submarine — torpedo.
Medjerda	1924	18-3-1941	Submarine — torpedo.
Tabaristan (V)	1914	29-5-1941	Submarine — torpedo.
Guelma	1928	17-7-1941	Submarine — torpedo.
Shahristan (VIII)	1938	29-7-1941	Submarine — torpedo.
Tunisia (II)	1927	4-8-1941	Aircraft — bombs.
Baluchistan (III)	1940	8-3-1942	Submarine — torpedo and shells.
Batna	1928	13-5-1942	Submarine — torpedo.
Arabistan (VIII)	1929	11-8-1942	Surface raider — gunfire.
Hamla	1929	23-8-1942	Submarine — torpedo.
Registan (IV)	1930	28-9-1942	Submarine — torpedo.
Bandar Shahpour	1927	30-4-1943	Submarine — torpedo.
Camerata (II)	1931	8-5-1943	Assault craft.

APPENDIX "D"

Vessels lost by shipwreck etc.

Name	Built	Date lost	How lost
Laristan	1896	22-10-1899	Sunk in collision.
Afghanistan (I)	1897	22-1-1904	Wrecked.
Goolistan	1898	10-9-1904	Sunk in collision.
Dwina	1862	24-11-1909	Sank after being partially submerged to act as landing stage.
Kurdistan	1906	20-10-1910	Foundered.
King Albert	1909	8-9-1915	Foundered after striking a submerged object.
Serbistan (1)	1896	11-1916	Disappeared.
Muristan (II)	1913	19-11-1916	Wrecked.
Kara (II)	1919	22-3-1920	Wrecked.
Mora	1922	8-2-1924	Wrecked.
Djerissa	1910	21-11-1927	Wrecked.
Thala	1928	8-2-1941	Wrecked.
Nigaristan (IV)	1912	24-9-1941	Abandoned on fire.
Floristan (I)	1928	19-1-1942	Wrecked.
Seistan (II)	1957	19-2-1958	Destroyed by explosion.

APPENDIX "E"

The following sequence of voyages, the last years of the M. V. AVRISTAN under the Strick flag, illustrate the "three cornered" nature of much of the trade after W.W.2. It was not all like this, however, as at least one vessel per month loaded in the Gulf for home.

AVRISTAN *Skyfotos*

Voyage 38. Loaded Glasgow, Manchester and Cardiff.

Port	Arrived	Sailed	Purpose
Cardiff		2140 22-1-61	Sailed with full general
Suez Canal	0600 5-2-61	2020 6-2-61	Canal transit
Aden	1200 12-2-61	2100 12-2-61	Fuel and water
Muscat	0130 18-2-61	1545 18-2-61	Discharged general
Dubai	2330 19-2-61	0545 23-2-61	Discharged general
Das Island	1900 23-2-61	1230 26-2-61	Discharged general
Bahrain	0600 27-2-61	1300 10-3-61	Discharged general
Mina al Ahmadi	1345 11-3-61	1645 13-3-61	Discharged general
Kuwait	2000 13-3-61	1400 27-3-61	Discharged general
Bahrain	1430 28-3-61	1300 31-3-61	Discharged general
Bushire	0600 1-4-61	1300 2-4-61	Discharged general

Umm Said	1200 3-4-61	0500 16-4-61	Discharged general
Bandar Shahpour	1800 17-4-61	1630 19-4-61	Discharged general
Basrah	0900 20-4-61	2200 26-4-61	Discharged (Sailed in ballast)
Karachi	1900 1-5-61	1030 7-5-61	Engine repairs
Mormugoa	0530 10-5-61	1100 31-5-61	Loaded iron ore
Suez Canal	1300 17-6-61	2230 18-6-61	Canal transit
Emden	1100 7-7-61	1300 9-7-61	Discharged iron ore
South Shields	0900 11-7-61		Drydock and refit

Voyage 39. Loaded Grangemouth, Middlesbrough and London.

Port	Arrived	Sailed	Purpose
London		1900 20- 9-61	Full general cargo
Suez Canal	0220 4-10-61	1730 5-10-61	Canal transit
Aden	0030 11-10-61	0700 12-10-61	Fuel and water. Loaded general and military cargo.
Salalah	2030 14-10-61	1300 16-10-61	Discharged military cargo
Muscat	0030 19-10-61	1600 20-10-61	Discharged general cargo
Bandar Abbas	1600 21-10-61	0600 25-10-61	Discharged general cargo
Dubai	1830 25-10-61	0700 28-10-61	Discharged general and military
Das Island	1900 28-10-61	1200 30-10-61	Discharged general
Bahrain	0230 31-10-61	0300 5-11-61	Discharged general
Kuwait	0230 6-11-61	1300 8-11-61	Discharged general
Bandar Shapour	0200 9-11-61	0800 10-11-61	Discharged general
Umm Said	2230 11-11-61	0800 16-11-61	Discharged general
Abu Dhabi	0200 17-11-61	1000 19-11-61	Discharged general
Umm Said	0530 20-11-61	1630 22-11-61	Discharged general
Basrah	1200 24-11-61	1800 30-11-61	Discharged (Sailed in ballast)
Port Louis (Mauritius)	1430 13-12-61	1930 29-12-61	Loaded full cargo sugar
Las Palmas	0130 27- 1-62	1400 28- 1-62	Fuel, water and stores.
Liverpool	1100 5-2-62	2200 19- 2-62	Discharged sugar. Loaded general

Voyage 40. Loaded general at Liverpool, Cardiff, Glasgow and Manchester.

Port	Arrived	Sailed	Purpose
Milford Haven	1430 18-3-62	1400 19-3-62	Loaded explosives
Suez Canal	1600 31-3-62	1630 1-4-62	Canal transit
Aden	1500 6-4-62	1700 7-4-62	Fuel, water. Loaded general
Muscat	0230 12-4-62	1330 13-4-62	Discharged general. and explosives
Das Island	0430 15-4-62	0700 16-4-62	Discharged general
Dammam	0130 18-4-62	1800 18-4-62	Discharged general
Bahrain	0100 19-4-62	0500 2-5-62	Discharged general and explosives
Kuwait	0630 3-5-62	0030 9-5-62	Discharged general and explosives
Dubai	2200 10-5-62	0130 13-5-62	Discharged general
Abu Dhabi	0930 13-5-62	1600 15-5-62	Discharged general
Umm Said	1130 16-5-62	0130 25-5-62	Discharged general
Dammam	1900 25-5-62	1830 29-5-62	Discharged general
Bushire	0930 30-5-62	0730 31-5-62	Discharged general
Basrah	1000 1-6-62	2200 5-6-62	Discharged (Sailed in ballast)
Durban	0530 26-6-62	1600 3-7-62	Loaded full cargo maize
Las Palmas	1430 26-7-62	1330 27-7-62	Fuel, water and stores
Belfast	1130 5-8-62	1300 11-8-62	Discharged maize
Rotterdam	2200 14-8-62	1330 9-9-62	Drydock and repairs

Voyage 41. Outwards from Rotterdam in ballast.

Port	Arrived	Sailed	Purpose
Tripoli (Lebanon)	0900 22-9-62	1430 30-9-62	Loaded full cargo 16″ pipe line.
Suez Canal	1330 1-10-62	2030 2-10-62	Canal transit
Aden	2100 7-10-62	1030 8-10-62	Fuel and water.
Abu Dhabi	1430 14-10-62	1800 24-10-62	Discharged pipes, sailed in ballast
Port Louis	0600 5-11-62	1330 10-11-62	Loaded full cargo sugar.
Las Palmas	1430 7-12-62	0830 8-12-62	Fuel and water.
Greenock	1800 17-12-62	2330 28-12-62	Discharged sugar, sailed in ballast

Voyage 42.

Port	Arrived	Sailed	Purpose
Antwerp	1700 1-1-63	0500 7-1-63	Loaded general cargo
London	0100 8-1-63	1100 26-1-63	Loaded general cargo
Suez Canal	0900 7-2-63	1730 8-2-63	Canal transit
Aden	1500 13-2-63	1630 15-2-63	Fuel and water. Loaded R.A.F. cargo
Salalah	0130 18-2-63	1730 19-2-63	Discharged R.A.F. cargo
Masirah Island	0730 21-2-63	1230 24-2-63	Discharged R.A.F. cargo
Muscat	0900 25-2-63	1130 28-2-63	Discharged general cargo
Dubai	1430 1-3-63	0000 3-3-63	Discharged general cargo
Abu Dhabi	0700 3-3-63	1700 4-3-63	Discharged general cargo
Jabal Dhanna	0800 5-3-63	1600 6-3-63	Discharged general cargo
Bahrain	1500 7-3-63	1330 11-3-63	Discharged general cargo
Kuwait	1700 12-3-63	1730 19-3-63	Discharged general cargo
Dammam	1430 20-3-63	0800 21-3-63	Discharged general cargo
Umm Said	0100 22-3-63	1500 26-3-63	Discharged general cargo
Basrah	0800 28-3-63	1700 31-3-63	Discharged (Sailed in ballast)
Port Elizabeth	0500 19-4-63	1900 27-4-63	Loaded full cargo maize
Las Palmas	2100 17-5-63	1630 18-5-63	Fuel and water
Manchester	1800 27-5-63		Discharged maize

AVRISTAN sold to Oriental Union Maritime Corp. (Liberian flag) Handed over at Manchester on 16-6-63. Renamed PAULIA.

APPENDIX

In the years prior to World War Two a weekly position sheet was issued by the Company to provide details of vessels employed in the coal trade to the Mediterranean. The ships loaded outwards at South Wales and North East Coast ports of the U.K. as well as Rotterdam and returned with iron ore.

ROTTERDAM & U.K.

C. P. DATED 1938	RATE	VESSEL		LATEST
18 January	6/-d	"HAMLA"	Passed	GIBRALTAR
17 January	6/6d	"GUELMA"	Passed	GIBRALTAR
18 January	6/-d	"TUNISIA"	Passed	GIBRALTAR
18 January	6/-d	"MARSA"	Passed	USHANT
18 January	6/-d	"LORCA"	Sails	ROTTERDAM
18 January	6/-d	"THALA"	Due	ROTTERDAM
18 January	6/-d	"MEDJERDA"	Sails	DAGENHAM
18 January	6/-d	"TAFNA"	Arrd	MIDDLESBRO'
18 January	6/-d	"CAMERATA"	Due	DAGENHAM
8 February	5/10½d	"BRIKA"	Due	TYNE
8 February	5/10½d	"KERMA"	Due	DAGENHAM

ALSO TO BE LOADED

FRIDAY 18TH FEBRUARY 1938

70

As can be seen, the entire fleet in early 1938 was employed in the transport of coal from Rotterdam to Genoa or Savona. This cargo was destined for the Italian State Railways and was a trade soon to be disrupted by war, never to return.

GENOA & SAVONA

REPORT	READY TO LOAD ROTTERDAM	CARGO ENG. TONS	ESTIMATE DUE GENOA/SAVONA	
5 Feb		6500	19 FEB	SAVONA
7 Feb		6475	21 Feb	SAVONA
8 Feb		6500	22 Feb	SAVONA
5 Feb		6450	23 Feb	SAVONA
9 Feb	LOADING	7050	1 Mar	SAVONA
8 Feb	18 Feb	6500	3 Mar	
21 Feb	22 Feb	6400	6/7 Mar	
8 Feb	23 Feb	6500	8/9 Mar	
20 Feb	23/24 Feb	7000	8/9 Mar	
27 Feb	4 Mar	6400	17/18 Mar	
2 Mar	4 Mar	6500	17/18 Mar	

CARGOES ROTTERDAM/GENOA-SAVONA
MARCH LOADING @ 5/10½d.

FRANK C. STRICK & CO. LIMITED
117/121, LEADENHALL STREET,
LONDON, E. C. 3.

ACKNOWLEDGEMENTS

The authors wish to thank the many people who have assisted in the preparation of this book and also the members of the Central Record Team of the World Ship Society who have helped in the research of the ship's histories and the flag and funnel colours.
The photographs were provided from many sources and where known are acknowledged in the history.
Thanks are also due to Messrs. S. Rabson, P. Barton, I. Buxton, J. Wright and the late L. Gray.

BALUCHISTAN *W.S.P.L.*

INDEX

THE STRICK COMPANIES

Frank C. Strick & Co. (founded 20.10.1885).
London & Paris Steamship Co. Ltd. (founded 1889)
(later became London & Paris Steamship & Investment Co. Ltd.)
Anglo-Algerian Steamship Co. Ltd. (founded 1889)
Anglo-Arabian & Persian Steamship Co. Ltd. (founded 1892)
Anglo-Algerian Steamship Co. (1896) Ltd.
The Dwina Ltd. (founded 1896)
La Commerciale Steam Navigation Co. Ltd. (founded 1905)
La Tunisienne Steam Navigation Co. Ltd. (founded 1909)
British Coaling Depots Ltd. (founded 1909)
Algiers Bunkering Co. Ltd.
Oran Coal Co. Ltd.
Strick, Scott & Co. Ltd. (founded 1911)
Iraq Produce Co. Ltd.
Strick Line Ltd. (founded 1.1.1913)
London, Paris & Marseilles Steamship Co. Ltd. (founded 1920)
Strick, Gorchs & Co. Ltd. (founded 1921)
North Devon Steamship Co. Ltd. (founded 1922)
Frank C. Strick & Co. (Busreh) Ltd. (founded 1923)
Shahristan Steamship Co. Ltd. (49% interest, acquired 1928)
Strick Line (1923) Ltd. (49% interest, acquired 1928)
Suez Canal Lighterage Co. Ltd. (49% interest, founded 1928)
Cory & Strick (Steamers) Ltd. (50% interest, founded 1928)
United Ship Supplies Ltd. (founded 1930)
Strick Line Ltd. (re-formed 1946)

also

Frank C. Strick & Co. (Cardiff) Ltd.
Frank C. Strick & Co. (Swansea) Ltd.
Frank C. Strick & Co. (Newport) Ltd.
Frank C. Strick & Co. (Newcastle) Ltd.
Frank C. Strick & Co. (Manchester) Ltd.
Frank C. Strick & Co. (Plymouth) Ltd.
Frank C. Strick & Co. (Glasgow) Ltd.
Frank C. Strick & Co. (South Wales) Ltd.
Frank C. Strick & Co. (Liverpool) Ltd.

1919
Sold
P & O

1928
Bought
Back
496